Garrison:

Thanks for everything
you do.

Take care.

How to Raise a Teenager Without Using Duct Tape

D1606384

How to Raise a Teenager Without Using Duct Tape

Jay Timms BMT MA CCC

This book is dedicated to fathers, but I hope that it will not just be fathers who read it. The principles set out here are applicable to fathers, mothers, aunts, uncles, grandparents...anyone who is involved in the raising of a teenager because, "It takes a village to raise a child".

This would not be possible without the loving support of my Bird, my Bud, and my Pea. You have taught me everything I know and you are the inspiration behind every event that has brought me to where I am today.

In Loving Memory of Dr. Gene Elmore. My mentor, my guide, and my friend. You are missed Gene.

Table of Contents

Introduction xi

Chapter 1: What Am I Doing Wrong? 1

Principle #1: Equality Within Reason 5
Principle #2: Coach to Caddie.. 6
Principle #3: Donkeys-R-Us.. 8
Principle #4: How to Mess Up Your Kids…But Only a Little Bit 11
Principle #5: The 4th Deadly Sin of Parenting Teens.................... 12
Principle #6: So What? 14
Summary 15

**Chapter 2: What's Up With All of These Emotional
Outbursts?** 17

Principle #1: Psychology 101... 20
Principle #2: Adult Brains vs. Adolescent Brains: And the winner is…! 22
Principle #3: The 3 "F" Words 24
Principle #4: Asking the Golden Question 27
Summary 28

Chapter 3: How Do I Calm Things Down in The House? 29

Principle #1: Triggers... 33
Principle #2: The Joker Effect 35
Principle #3: Soothing the savage beast....................................... 37
Principle #4: The Law of the Coca-Cola Bottle 40
Principle #5: Being positive about the "negative" emotions 42
Summary 44

Chapter 4: What Do My Kids REALLY Need? 45

Principle #1: The Velcro Theory 48
Principle #2: Holding it Together from the Beginning 49
Principle #3: How to Make the Velcro Stick 51
Principle #5: When the Velcro Doesn't Stick 55
Summary: 57

Chapter 5: How do I have an effective and meaningful conversation with my teen? 59

Principle #1: I Feel Like I'm Talking to a Brick Wall! 62
Principle #2: Effective Listening 64
Principle #3: Cost Benefit Analysis (CBA) 76
Principle #4: When the Bad Goes Really Bad 78
Summary 80

Chapter 6: How Do I Effectively Discipline My Teenager? 81

Principle #1: What Works and What Doesn't 84
Principle #2: Boot Camp 85
Principle #2: The Opossum 89
Principle #3: Bowling for Dummies 92
Principle #4: Deal Or No Deal? 94
Principle #5: Bouncing Them Back 97
Summary 101

Chapter 7: Am I doing a good job as a parent? 103

Principle #1: Compassion 106
Principle #2: Honesty 108
Principle #3: I'm Sorry 111
Principle #4: Real Men Wear Pink 113
Summary 114

Chapter 8: Summary to the Summary of the Summaries 115

Why Is This Book in Your Hands?

How many times have I heard "Teens don't come with an instruction manual"? Almost every time I've had a parent in my office. Chances are that if you're reading this, you've heard this or said it yourself. You just want to understand how to fix this thing that appears to be broken. How do you make it work? Well, hopefully you'll find some answers here.

Whenever I sit down with new clients, I give a little disclaimer about what they're about to experience, so I'm going to do the same for you. I tend to be pretty straightforward. I'm not writing this to appease anyone or make ugly things seem pretty. I can almost guarantee that there are things here that you will not agree with. I have opinions and I'm fully aware that other people may have opposing ones. That's the beauty of humanity. We can all see one individual object a million different ways depending on our point of view. It's not my intention to offend anyone, but I know it's possible and I'm willing to live with the consequences.

I also want to point out a bias that will be present throughout this book. I have written this for Moms, Dads, Aunts, Uncles, Grandmas, Grandpas, Foster parents…the list goes on. If you are in some way taking care of a child, the principles here will apply. Having said that, in working with families I have noticed a distinct lack of information out there for dads of teens. Because of that, I have spent time preparing thoughts specifically for dads here in this book. Many of the examples that I use in this book will be specifically for dads or about dads. These examples are not used to set men apart from women in the roles of raising children but in fact, the intent is to close the gap between men and women that is present in much of the literature and research about parents and teens. It may also provide moms with some ideas of what dads may be feeling and how to engage dad more in the process.

One of the main reasons for writing this book in this format is that there aren't really many books specifically intended to help fathers interact with their teenagers. Most of the books out there are supposedly for parents, but if you read them it becomes painfully obvious that the books are written for moms. Most of the books out there for parents of teens tend to miss some of the important aspects about parenting from a father's point of view. Ask for a book specifically for fathers and their teenage children at your local bookstore and you'll be greeted with a confused look in response. Lots of information exists on fathers of young children, but not so much on fathers of teens. Also, most of the information out there says that fathers are essentially not as good at parenting as mothers. I don't agree with this at all. Too many times fathers are left out of the conversation because of the assumption that they don't want to be involved or have no clue what they're doing. This is an unfortunate mistake and I'm going to offer another point of view.

The second reason for writing this book is that most of the information out there is weighed down with heavy theory and jargon. I don't know about you, but I don't have time to wade through a bunch of words. That's why this book is short and to the point and will hopefully begin to bridge the gap. Think of it as a reference guide that you can use again and again when you find yourself dealing with raising your teen.

So here it is. A no nonsense approach on how to deal with your teens. I trust you will like it.

Introduction

Over my many years of working with parents and being one, I have come to one basic and fundamental truth:

Being an effective parent is something that is really backwards. It is without a doubt the most daunting, responsibility-laden job that we will ever have. And we have had no training on how to do it.

Being an effective parent takes time, energy, money, focus, and control. We need to be able to manage all of these things effectively to fulfill our multiple responsibilities as parents, providers, and members of the community. But nobody taught us how to do this. If this was a real job, we would expect that the employer would provide us with a detailed list of responsibilities that we are expected to fulfill, and training to sharpen our skills in preparation for the first day. We would also expect the employer to be around when we had questions about what to do. I don't know about you, but as a dad I never went through **that** training process. It feels like I am at a job where they said, "Welcome. You're hired. Now get to work". I would have quit the next day if this was a job I was hired for. No question.

So what is it that makes us stick around (aside from the fact that there is no box laying around to return the teens to the manufacturer)?

Instinct.

We as human beings have a basic, fundamental urge to give to the next generation. Yes, love plays a huge part in why we don't quit but research shows that this urge to leave some sort of legacy is so strong that it often blinds us to many other things that need our attention. Unfortunately for many of us that same instinct is missing a key ingredient: understanding how to do the job that we are driven to do. How frustrating!

I remember the first day that I met Dave. I had been working with his 14-year-old son Mike for about two months and had met with his wife Susan many times. The topic of conversation with Mike was always the same: "My dad and I always fight and I think he hates me." Susan described Dave as a great guy who loved his kids more than anything in the world, but who also had a fast temper and an inability to relate to his emotional teenage kids.

I think Dave was a bit skeptical of me. I haven't met too many dads who jump at the chance to talk to me about their feelings, then turn around and pay me like I'm doing them a favor. I'm sure that Susan kept telling Dave about the work we were trying to do together with Mike, but I was never able to get a hold of him. I kept trying to get Dave to come into my office and there were a few times when he agreed, but something always came up. One day I decided that I needed to meet him so I showed up at his home at about dinnertime. As I stood on the doorstep waiting like some cheesy salesman, I heard Susan trying to convince Dave to open the door for me, explaining who I was. I don't think he was impressed. When he did let me in, he sat in his easy chair, arms folded, with a scowl on his face.

He let me speak for about 5 minutes and then said something that I've heard time and time again: "Well, to be honest the problem is not our relationship, it's the fact that my kids have no respect for me. I work my tail off for them every day and they don't listen to me when I tell them something. The people who work for me listen and respect me. I tell you, when I was a kid, if I had done or said half of the things my kids get away with, my dad would have shot me with a shotgun. Other kids respect their dads, but not mine. Maybe there's something wrong with me, and maybe this is all my fault. Maybe I do suck as a father. I just know that I can't control my own kids".

And this is how most of my conversations with parents begin. The truth of the matter is, Dave was right. His kids didn't respect him. No matter how much he loved them and they loved him, no matter what he did at work and how successful he was, he didn't get it. He didn't understand that there is so much more to being a dad than having your kids listen to you when you want them to. He had the desire, but the practical knowledge or the "how to" was missing. Honestly though, have any of us really been taught specifically how to be a parent? If so, I missed that class in school. Had Dave failed? No, absolutely not.

Parents come to me for a lot of different reasons. They're told to come by their spouses, they're sick of yelling at their teens, their relationships and jobs are suffering, they're afraid that their kids are going to wind up doing something really stupid if they can't control them better...the list goes on. All in all, there are basically seven questions that every parent who comes to see me asks:

1) **What am I doing wrong?**

2) **Why is my kid so emotional?**

3) **How do I keep peace in my house?**

4) **What is behind the behaviours and what do they REALLY need?**

5) **How do I have an effective and meaningful conversation with my teen?**

6) **How do I discipline my teen in a way that actually works?**

7) **Am I doing a good job as a parent?**

In each of the following chapters, I'm going to tackle one of those questions. I'll give you practical tools that you can use right now to change your relationship with your teen. Maybe you could consider this as the instruction manual that didn't get shipped with your teen.

Chapter 1: What Am I Doing Wrong?

"Dealing with teenagers is such a warm and fuzzy time of life isn't it? We used to play on the playground, but now all we do is play in the mood swings."

-Author unknown.

Honestly? Probably not much. Seriously. Here you are, sitting and reading a book on how to get closer to your teens. This is a great start and it says something good about who you are. What's wrong is that most parents see the problem as bigger than it actually is. When parents come into my office, more often than not they say, "Jay, this is THE biggest challenge that I have ever come up against. I don't know how to deal with this." The anxiety that comes up for parents when they say, "I don't know what to do" actually makes it tougher for them to deal with their problems. For dads this is especially difficult. We're guys. If it's broken, let's fix it. If we don't know how to fix it, it causes us stress. So, your problem is not really the problem. The problem is the way that you're looking at it.

I ride a motorcycle. I love riding my bike. When I'm riding, there are three pairs of glasses that I carry with me. When it's bright and sunny, I wear dark sunglasses. When it's foggy out or twilight, I wear my yellow lenses. When it's night, I wear my clear lenses. Why would I carry three pairs of glasses? Obviously because each one of them changes my view, or alters how I see things. The lenses that cover our eyes skew our vision. As parents, we have a pair of glasses that we wear when we look at our teens. Whether or not we put these glasses on consciously, we see our teens through them consistently.

Most parents see their teens through one type of glasses. Often parents will say that their teens are moody, disobedient, challenging, withdrawn, etc. If these are the glasses that you have on, imagine your teen coming in at the end of the day and throwing himself into a chair giving a big sigh. Immediately, if you are seeing your child through these lenses, what would you think? Probably something like, "Oh no. Here we go. What am I going to have to deal with now, because he's moody, disobedient, challenging, withdrawn, etc."? Now, if you were wearing a different pair of glasses, you may ask yourself, "Wow! That was quite a sigh! I wonder if he was just was running home from the bus, or if it's just because he had a bad day?" Most parents, however, will start with the first pair of glasses, and have a distorted view of what's really going on.

Why do so many parents see their teens this way? Truth be told, we see them this way because it's true. Sometimes they ARE moody, disobedient, challenging, withdrawn, etc. But sometimes they're not. Let me ask a question: do you have any friends or partners that you know of who are moody, disobedient, challenging, withdrawn, etc? Think about the people you work with. Think about the people that you deal with on a daily basis. Of course you know people like that! We all do. Imagine if you were with this person at work. This person starts complaining and whining about something that you did or didn't do. Can you imagine yourself saying, "Don't you dare talk to me like that! You know what? I'm sick of listening to you complain and moan! You think YOU have it tough? Spend a day in my job. Life is tough. Get over it. Until you can control yourself, I want you to go to your office and just spend some time thinking about it. When you're ready, you can come out and we'll discuss it. Until then, just shut up and go away!" No, you probably wouldn't talk to them like that. So why don't you treat them the way that you treat your teen? There are probably a lot of reasons, but when you look at the adults in your life, you see them through different lenses. You see them as your equal in society (generally speaking). When it comes to our children, we don't normally see them as our equals.

Principle #1: Equality Within Reason

What we need to do is to change the lenses we look at our teens through and see our teens as equals. I said that in a seminar once and a parent blurted out, "You mean I'm supposed to treat my teenager, who treats me like crap, like an equal?" Well, yes and no. I mean within reason. I mean equality within reason. I will get into this in a bit more detail as we go further along, but let me explain it a bit now. We naturally see our teens as less than us. From birth to age ten, we could say, "Do it", and more often than not our kids would listen. When they were toddlers, you could say, "Look. That pretty sun is purple" and they would think, "Okay, I guess the color of the sun is purple just because dad or mom said so". Now that they're older, they don't react well to that any more because they're more able to think for themselves. Again, I'll talk more about that in Chapter 2.

Up to this point, our teens have generally listened to us so we naturally assume that they'll continue to do so. Nothing has changed on our end, so our children should continue to react the same way as before, right? All of a sudden there's this shift where they aren't listening and obeying quite as quickly as they used to (if at all). And we get frustrated when they don't. By the way, that word "frustrated" is THE biggest word I hear when I speak to parents. It's not mad, it's not sad, it's not tired. It's, "I'm frustrated!" We get frustrated when they don't communicate with us. Let's be honest here. Would you communicate with someone who came up to you and said, "Do it now! Because I said so!" I sure wouldn't. In part, I don't blame teens for not communicating with their parents. The challenge that we have as parents is that we need to shift the way that we see our teens because although nothing has changed on our end, there is a major change that is happening on theirs.

Principle #2: Coach to Caddie

I'm a bit of a golfer. Not a great one, but I like to swing the clubs every once in a while. Personal life aside, one of the greatest stories in golf is Tiger Woods. When he was growing up and learning how to golf, who taught him? His dad did. As a coach, I'm assuming that when Tiger was practicing, as he was lining up, his dad would say something like, "Okay. So what you want to do is you need to get your legs a little bit farther apart here and bend your knees. Pretend you're squatting. Good. Now when your arms come back, make sure that your front arm stays straight and that your hips lead your arms. That's where you'll get the momentum." Every step of the way his dad would guide him. And Tiger was saying something like, "Okay. That makes sense", thinking, "well, I guess so because Dad said so". Now, when Tiger got older and started to play professionally, where was his coach? He was on the sidelines. Tiger doesn't have someone standing over his shoulder on every swing on the course telling him what to do.

Tiger isn't left to his own devices however. He has a caddie. A caddie's job is to be there when the golfer needs his opinion. To increase his value, a caddie will know the course ahead of time and be aware of the dangers, traps, and possible barriers that the golfer may encounter along the way. That way, if Tiger says, "what do you think" the caddie can say, "well, to be honest with you, I've been on this course before and this is what I'm seeing." Tiger Woods could say, "Okay, sounds great" or "I don't agree". The caddie will then stand back and let Tiger play the game.

Can you imagine, at The Masters Tournament, Tiger Woods lines up and is about to go into his backswing and all of a sudden his caddie yells out, "Wait! Stop! What are you doing? I can't believe you're doing it like that! I've told you a million times that you're doing it wrong! Why don't you ever listen to me? And don't you DARE argue with me! You keep your mouth shut!" That would be the shortest career ever for a caddie.

Our job as parents is exactly the same. We need to move from coach, which is what we have done for the first 10 or so years, to caddie. We need to move from saying to our children, "No don't. If you touch the stove you will get burned. Stop", to "well, it is up to you". My school-aged daughter hears, "no, don't" a lot. Not that she listens all the time, but with my teenage son I can't do that anymore. My job as a parent is to stand back and say, "Look. Here are the options that I see for you. Here is what I think you should do", *but only if he says, "Hey dad, what do you think?"* I need to change the way that I am teaching my son. Instead of "Listen to me", I need to stand back and say, "Hum. What do you think about this one? Where are we going to go with this? Figure it out and I am here to help you if you need it."

Why is it so important to move from coach to caddie? Well, how do you learn things in life? You learn through experience. You can tell me all you want what it tastes like to drink a fine Californian Cabernet wine, but I don't drink wine. I never have. I have no idea what it tastes like. I used to be a bartender and run restaurants so I know all of the "buzz words", but I've never tasted it. "Oh, it's buttery with fruity notes and an oak finish…" I have no idea why people would drink the stuff. A pad of butter with fruit and bark going down my throat sounds pretty unappealing to me. But if I experience it, it makes sense. So for our teens to truly grow, we have to let them experience things. We have to let them go out and do things that normally would have us saying, "AHHH! Don't!" We're afraid because we want to hold on. Our teens don't want us to hold on, and really, we aren't doing them any good. What you're going to find is that the tighter you hold on, the more they're going to fight to get away.

I really want you to keep this in your mind as you're dealing with your teens. If you do nothing else with this book aside from remembering this one piece, I will be happy. Remember, you're not a coach anymore. You're the caddie. You cannot protect your children and demand that they listen to you the way they did when they were younger. They're changing and we as parents need to change with them. This is really tough for most parents to try to wrap their heads around. They are NOT going to listen to you if you try to hold them back and restrict them. You didn't listen to your parents when they did it to you, so why do you think your kids are any different? You're there to help them make the tough decisions in life, letting them learn through their experiences, not through yours. You're there to support them, not lead them. You're the perfect person to help them do this because you HAVE walked the course before. You DO know what it's like. Even though your teen thinks you have no clue, we both know you do. But they need to be able to figure things out with you as their caddie, not as their coach.

Principle #3: Donkeys-R-Us

I want to follow this up a little by talking about what it feels like for your teen to have you trying to be their coach. There is a principle I call the "Donkeys-R-Us" principle. This basically states that if you grab a donkey by the face and the reins and try to pull the donkey along, what's going to happen? It's going to dig in its heels and fight you. Now, I'm not a farmer but I do know that if you want a donkey to follow you, you have to come along side the donkey and walk with it. You can't pull a donkey. That's where the phrase "stubborn as a mule" comes from. The same thing is true with your teens. You have to come along side your teens and walk with them and experience life with them. I will talk more about how to do this in the coming chapters, but we have to be willing to let them experience life! Let them go out and get their hearts broken. Let them date the looser so that they understand the difference between a good boyfriend and a bad boyfriend.

Yes, I know as a parent you're thinking, "How can I let them go out and get hurt like that?" Have you ever had your heart broken? Of course you have. I was a geek in high school and so became quite an expert and my heart being broken. What does that do for you to have your heart broken? It adds experience. I'm not suggesting that we open the door and say, "Go for it because you need to experience life". There are some limits that we will talk about in the coming chapters, but for now, understand that it's actually okay for your teen to get hurt every once in a while. Always remember that there's a huge difference between making people grow and letting people grow.

In 1994, there was a movie called "Little Giants". In the movie, there's a mom that is absolutely paranoid about protecting her son. He's a scrawny little guy who wears glasses and has asthma. In the movie he puffs his inhaler like a chain smoker smokes cigarettes. They live in a really small neighborhood with a football team that all of the kids want to play on. This boy is no different. He wants to play really badly. In one scene, the kids are all practicing together and the coach is off in the corner of the field cheering them on. In the middle of the practice, all of the kids stop what they're doing and look up in the same direction. The screen pans over to this little guy walking towards the field. He has on his helmet with his glasses jammed in the facemask, but as the shot gets wider you see that his mom has wrapped him up in pillows and mattresses and duct tape along with all of his padding. He looks like the Michelin man as he struggles to walk towards this field of glory that he wants to be on. His mom really doesn't want him to get hurt, so she tries to protect him.

Now I've played and coached football and I know that it hurts. At the end of the day, what did this kid learn? He learned that football doesn't hurt. He was so protected he could have been hit by a semi-truck and he would have just bounced off of it. So what happens when the padding comes off (and it will) and he does get hurt? The reality of "football doesn't hurt" is false. It isn't real so it comes as a real shock. As parents, protecting our teens is our job, but not allowing them to get hurt is actually detrimental to their emotional and spiritual growth.

Here's another movie: "Finding Nemo". If you have teens, you probably saw this movie when they were younger. There's one part in it that exemplifies what I believe is wrong with trying to shelter our teens. Marlin and Dory have been swallowed by the whale, and they're both reacting to it very differently. Dory is floating along enjoying the ride, while Marlin is fighting to get out. As he bangs his head on the inside of the whale he keeps saying, "I have to get out! I have to find my son! I have to tell him how old... sea... turtles... are!" At this point, he sobs and floats down onto the tongue of the whale. Dory comes down and says, "There, there. It's alright. It'll be okay." Marlin says, "No, you don't understand. I have to find him! I promised I would never let anything happen to him". Dory pauses and says, "Huh. Well that's a funny thing to promise." Marlin looks stunned and says, "Huh?" Dory continues, "Well, you can't never let *anything* happen to him. Then nothing would *ever* happen to him... not much fun for little Harpo".

Unfortunately the wisdom of a little blue fish with short-term memory loss is something that many parents miss. We have to let our kids experience life, because without experience, how can they be prepared for what's to come? You're not going to be able to protect them for the rest of their life, so I wonder, when do you plan on letting them go? When you are dead? "Not much fun for little Harpo".

Now, in all honesty, this is harder to accomplish that it sounds. "Just let go". I'm not stupid enough to believe that it's as simple as that. It's not that easy to just let go. All of a sudden the fears and worries take over and you wonder, "Is my son or daughter going to be okay". Parents will often say to me, "Well, if I let go, what if they get into a situation where they could really get hurt like drugs, or gangs, or the sex trade?" Fair enough. At times we absolutely have to step in, and in the following chapters I will speak to how you can do that in a way that expresses your concerns. Generally speaking though, recognize that if you hold on to your teen too tightly, you may be doing them more harm than good.

Principle #4: How to Mess Up Your Kids…But Only a Little Bit

I teach parents how to be better parents, but if you take a couple of minutes with my kids and wife they will tell you that, I'm far from perfect. None of us are perfect. None of us have been trained to raise teens and this is sometimes the biggest revelation that teens hear from me. When I say, "You know, your parents really have no clue what they're doing. They're just faking it", often kids almost fall off their chair. Think about it though. We are faking it! All of us are! As I said in the intro, none of us have been taught how to be a parent. Again, if we were taught, I missed that day of school. People can argue that your own parents are the greatest teachers of how to parent effectively. In some ways, I totally agree with that. I have great parents, and although they have made some mistakes, they definitely taught me how to raise a son like Jay Timms. The problem is that I don't have a son like Jay Timms. I have a son and a daughter, but neither of them are Jay Timms. I never got the lessons on how to raise them. They're totally different from me in many ways.

When my son comes into the room and lies to me and I make a poor choice of words in response, I think to myself afterward that I probably shouldn't have approached it the way I did. But I did. We all do it. I think our job as parents is to try to do as little damage to our teen's psyche as possible. All of us, and I mean ALL of us are messed up a little because of our parents. They did it to us, now it's our turn to do it to our teens. In saying that, our job is to try to mess them up as little as we can. Once we realize that this is going to happen, that we're going to mess our kids up and we come to terms with it, it actually relieves a lot of pressure. As a wise person once said, "There is no one way to be a perfect parent, but there are a million ways to be a good one." You're not going to be perfect so stop trying to be and enjoy the ride.

Principle #5: The 4th Deadly Sin of Parenting Teens

There is a really important topic that I want to discuss that fits in here. Dr. John Gottman is often considered by many experts to be *the* leading expert in North America on relationships. Now his work is with men and women in intimate relationships, but in my eyes all relationships are relationships. Throughout this book, I will be bringing up Gottman and his research because after having received training in his theories, I consider it groundbreaking in the field of relationships.

In the 70's, Dr. Gottman started researching relationships. He wanted to know if he could predict who would get divorced and who would actually stay together as a couple. After thirty plus years of watching couples, Dr. Gottman can successfully predict divorce with over ninety percent accuracy within fifteen minutes of meeting the couple. Now, you have to understand something: in psychology, if we can predict something ten percent of the time, we consider that to be something of worth. Dr. Gottman has over ninety percent accuracy.

So what does that have to do with you and your teenager? It's how Gottman and people who work with him and who are trained Gottman therapists can help you. Gottman has found that there are 4 things that predict divorce. Out of those 4, the most toxic and harmful to relationships (remember relationships are relationships whether it is you and your partner or you and your teen) is something called contempt.

Contempt is an attitude that conveys superiority to the other person. It is in effect saying, "How can you be that stupid? If you were as good as me you wouldn't do that". It usually comes out as sarcasm and mockery, or the ever- demeaning eye rolling. You know when a person rolls their eyes at you that they're thinking, "You've got to be kidding me!"

I've worked with families who use sarcasm as their main communication tool. When they're confronted about it, I often hear, "I'm just kidding! Lighten up a little!" Unfortunately, this form of "kidding" is degrading and can do some serious harm to your relationships. With your children, it's easy to have contempt. I mean, really, we're superior to them, right? Well, yes and no. We have more experience, a greater depth of knowledge, and are the ones who make the rules. Unfortunately, this does not make us superior. Gottman says that the use of contempt creates a "distancing cascade".

What's a distancing cascade? Well let's assume that I walked up to you and for no reason punched you in the arm. It hurts. Aside from the fact that you would probably hit me back, let's assume that I came at you again and hit you again. You might shy away a bit this time. If I came at you the third time, you would try to get away before I even came close. It's the same thing with relationships and communication. If our children come to us looking for help and we hit them with contempt, it hurts. If this is the response that we give them time and time again, they will be less and less likely to come back. Nobody wants to be treated like an idiot, so nobody in their right mind is going to go looking for it. That distancing becomes bigger and bigger, and all the while we as parents are trying to hold on tighter to our kids and control our teens. What are they doing as they are being emotionally assaulted? Trying to get away as fast and as far as they can. So as you can see, the attitude of superiority with your teens is one that will push your child away faster than it will help them to stay on the "straight and narrow".

Principle #6: So What?

So what? Well, sometimes the toughest part about growing up is waiting for your parents to let you do it. Now, just for a second, think about when you were a teenager. None of us are so old that we don't remember that far back, regardless of what our teens think. So, as a teenager, what did you want? Did you want your parents to be around you all the time? Did you want your parents to be all over you and watching everything you did and pushing you to be a "better person". Of course not! You just wanted them to BACK OFF! I don't care if it was in the 40's, 50's, 60's, 70's, 80's, or whenever it was. We wanted our parents to go away and relax a bit. And yet somehow we think that our kids are different?

Probably the greatest comment I heard about this came from a teenage girl who was sitting in the room with her mom and dad during a family counseling session. She was fed up with her parents, especially her mom who was constantly nagging her about everything from the way she dressed to the way she prepared her lunch in the morning. Her mom had just finished a tirade when this girl turned to her mom and said, "You know mom, I wish you would just get a life! You have already been a teenager. Why don't you get out of my life and get your own!" I thought, "Good for her!" because really, it's the truth. Sometimes we as parents need to go out and get our own lives.

I heard a story that at one point early in his career, Tiger Woods was standing on a course and was really struggling with what to do next. His dad asked him, "So where do you want the ball to go?" Tiger said, "Over there" pointing to the green. Tiger's dad said, "Okay, now figure out how to get it there". It would be so much easier for us as parents to just get out there and do it for our kids. It would save us all grief and heartache because we could probably do it quicker and with less mess than our teens could do it. But we can't.

As parents, we need to be able to step back a little and let our children experience their lives so that they can learn and grow into mature adults who turn around and mess up their teens. But just a little bit.

Summary

- The way that you choose to see your teen will alter your view (positively or negatively) of everything that they do. Highlight that word "choose" because it is a choice. You CHOOSE how you see your teen.

- Your teens will distance themselves when they feel disrespected. Does this mean that we have to dance around and try to not make them upset? No! Make them upset! I think more teens need to be mad at their parents because it means parents are setting boundaries. But respecting the teen is something totally different.

- Sarcasm is not the way to motivate. Guilt is not the way to motivate. You may have a better perspective than they do, but don't rub it in their faces.

- You have no idea what you're doing. Get over it and move on.

- We need to move from coach to caddie. You can't raise your teens the way you've raised them for the first 10 years of their lives so don't even try.

- You're not the one playing the game. You're there to help them see the green and then step back and let them get the ball there.

Chapter 2: What's Up With All of These Emotional Outbursts?

When I speak with parents about their teens, most often the word that they use is "frustrating". Sometimes we have a really hard time understanding their emotions and behaviours. They make no sense whatsoever and often leave us asking, "What just happened?" In fact, we often don't distinguish between emotions and behaviours. We just call them "behaviours". "My child needs to change his/her behaviour." Most often when I work with families with teens and I sit down with the parents and ask them what's going on for them, they say, "My kid's behaviour is just horrible! It's just really bad". Then when I sit down with the teens and get their perspective, more often than not they're just emotional. Their emotions are so out of whack that even *they* don't know what's going on for them. So we don't even have an effective vocabulary to describe what our teens are doing. We just call it "behaviour". It is really important for parents to understand what's happening, both inside the brains of their teens, but also what's happening for themselves during these frequent "fights". And 99% of the time it begins with emotions for both of you.

Principle #1: Psychology 101

This is the only part of theory that you will find in this book so bare with me here. Do you have any idea what happens inside your brain and the brains of your teens when you get emotional? Most people don't. If you look at the brain, there are 2 parts that are really important in functioning in our daily lives. The first part is called the "limbic system". If we were to draw a line through the head behind the temples and another line through your nose to the back of your head, the crosshairs of those lines would be where in the brain the limbic system is. This limbic system has a series of different organs in it with big names like the hippocampus, the amygdala and other names that really mean nothing to most people. What's important is that this is the part of your brain that is in charge of emotions. Every emotion that you feel originates from this part of the brain: happiness, sadness, anger, fear, etc. It all happens here. We will call it the "emotion center". We actually share this part of our brains with every animal on the planet. I have a little dog that basically sits in the corner and shakes all day named Doby. Doby gets nervous when he's outside and a leaf blows by him. He has this emotional center. And you know it because when you slam your hand down on the counter or make a loud noise, he jumps and just shakes harder.

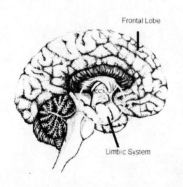

Frontal Lobe

Limbic System

The other part of the brain that is important in dealing with daily life is the part of the brain that goes from our forehead back to almost the crown of your head. This is called the frontal lobe or "thinking center". This is the part of our brains that makes us uniquely human. This part helps us to plan, organize, think logically, and dissect information. It is a very important part of how we function at home, at school, at work, and even at the local Starbucks as we figure out what concoction we're going to drink.

What's important to understand about the brain is that when the emotion center in our brain is highly activated, the thinking center cannot function at all. It shuts down. In other words, when we're emotional we can't think logically. I'll come back to this in a minute, but this one principle is probably THE most important piece of information that you can ever have in dealing with your teens:

Remember that if there is emotion involved, you cannot think straight and neither can they.

Why does this happen to people? Why is it that when the emotion center in our brain is highly charged that the thinking center of our brain shuts down? Think about it. Let's say you're coming home from a movie one night and your car breaks down so you have to walk the rest of the way. You're in an area of town that really doesn't have the best reputation and you find yourself walking through an alley with little to no light. As you walk, you hear a loud BANG coming from behind you. What would you do? If the thinking center was functioning at this point, you may think something like "Wow, that was loud. I wonder what that was? It sounded kind of like a piece of metal that hit concrete. It couldn't have been wood because it wouldn't have made such a hard sound..." Of course you wouldn't be thinking that! By then you would be dead. You would have probably jumped and spun around to see what was going on. In a split second, your mind shut down the logical part of your brain, increased your heart rate, dilated your pupils so that you could see better, decreased the production of stomach juices, and increased your blood flow. And it took as long as it takes you to read the word "B A N G!" It's an instinctual survival tactic.

Principle #2: Adult Brains vs. Adolescent Brains: And the winner is…!

So far I have been speaking as if the adult brain and the adolescent's brains are equal. Now, I don't think that many parents would suggest that their brains and their child's brains are equal, but do you realize just how unequal they are? Did you know that from the time a child is eleven to twelve years old until they are twenty to twenty-three years old that their brains will increase in size by one third? That means that as an average adult, your brain is one third bigger than your adolescent child's brain. Not surprised? Okay, do you want to know which part is missing? Research shows that the part of the brain that grows during this time period is the thinking center. That means that the part of the brain that is missing during this time period for your teens is the part of the brain that assists in thinking, reason, planning ahead, and foresight into the consequences of actions. That means that your child's actions are generally run by emotion, habits, and limited insights. (Usually at this point in my seminars, light bulbs will start going off over the heads of the parents I speak to.) That's the reason why parents look at each other and say things like, "What the heck was she thinking?" Guess what? They weren't! They can't! This is also why when you ask your son or daughter, "Do you have any idea what you have just done to yourself?" you get a blank stare back. Your teens actually don't know what they have just done to themselves because they don't have the ABILITY to think things through fully at this point in their lives and so will do stupid things. They have to wait for this grey stuff up front to fully develop.

There is no question that one of the reasons that teenagers are so emotional is their hormones. These are some powerful chemicals that do strange and weird things to the body. But the other side is that your teen is trying to figure out how to deal with a totally new environment. Picture something for second. Imagine that aliens came to this planet and took you back to their planet. You heard rumors that once you get to this planet you will have everything you would ever want. You will have freedoms beyond measure like being able to eat ice cream at ten in the morning without someone telling you that you can't, you will find happiness, and have the ability to access material things that you have always wanted. Sounds pretty good, doesn't it? It would be, but there's only one problem. They're going to put you in a totally new body, one you have never experienced before. This new body will do things that your old body never did. You will feel things that you have never felt, see things that you never thought possible, and feel this new body shift in ways that you never thought possible. And this will last for about five years. Have fun.

This might be bearable if it was only the body that was different. But it isn't. You didn't have a "real" brain up to this point. And the part that you were lacking is the part that allows for the ability to plan ahead, see consequences and possibilities. Can you imagine that these aliens now implant new parts into your brain that allows you to see how much you have missed out on living on that other dull, boring planet? What would you want to do? That's right. You would want to go out and experience it all. NOW! It's like being given the key to the bank and being told, "Yah sure. Take whatever you want." No wonder teenagers look at their parent who is acting like the coach saying, "No you can't do that" to them, they rebel. This is some cool stuff I'm experiencing and someone is saying "No you can't"? Whatever!

Teens go off and do stupid things or have bad "behaviour" (remember it may not be just a behaviour) for three reasons: a) their brains are not fully developed, b) they have begun to realize that the world they have lived in up until now is actually quite limiting and they develop opinions about your rules, and c) the emotions they're experiencing are new and they have a hard time dealing with the intensity of them. So the next time you're dealing with a teen who appears to be going nuts, maybe this will help you to have a little more compassion for the circumstance that they are facing. Being a teen sucks. I'm glad I'm not there anymore!

Principle #3: The 3 "F" Words

Here is one of my ADHD tangents. Did you know that your body and brain really can't distinguish between the strong emotions of sadness and anger? It can't tell the difference between frustrated and scared either. Our body just knows that it is feeling something strongly and reacts to it. Our body goes into a naturally defensive state and we get ready to protect ourselves. This happens in three ways: Fight, Flight, and Freeze.

Fight

Most people will understand what I mean when I say "fight", but what may surprise many people is the way that this response shows its' face in real-life situations. Fighting can be termed as any response that is intended to either shock or intimidate the source of the perceived threat in an effort to stop the attack. Take a second and think about a dog. Imagine a dog being backed into a corner. When a dog prepares to fight, it bares its teeth, the hair on its back stands up and it starts to growl. You can see the muscles in its legs flexing, ready to pounce. So now think about a person whose response to a strong emotion is to fight. This is the one response that is most often associated with men in society. You may imagine fists flying, yelling, screaming, slamming doors, walls, etc. And you would be right, but there is actually more to it.

Fighting from a parents' point of view does not have to be a physical thing. In speaking with teens, some will describe a response that has nothing to do with yelling or screaming. One teen said, "It's like, I know he's pissed off, but he doesn't yell like he normally does. He just gets this look on his face like he's kind of smiling, and then he starts ripping me apart. Like, he just totally lets go and comes up with stuff that's just awful. Sometimes it hurts a lot more than if he actually was hitting me. Words just stay longer". What's happening is that the father is reacting to the emotions he's feeling and is trying to actively push the source of those emotions away. Again, more often than not, fighting is a response that most people can relate to.

In teens, often the fight response may come out as aggressive or disobedient behaviours. Parents will often say that their children need anger management classes. Well, actually what they need is to be able to get the perceived threat off of their back, so they're just trying to shock or intimidate the threat in an effort to get a break.

Flight

Think of that dog in the corner again. Sometimes animals won't attack, but will actually retreat. Even if they're backed into a corner, they look for a way out. I've seen some animals that are quite ingenious with the ways that they get out of a situation (when I was a kid, cats didn't like me very much). Ironically, I've also seen some men who are quite skilled at getting out of emotional situations. Some men are a little more subtle about it and hide behind words like, "working late", "very busy", "responsibility", and "down time". They will come up with anything to not go home and deal with all of the emotions of being the father of a teen, and rightfully so. The emotions involved in parenting a teen are intense and no sane person would want to stand in that emotional waterfall and say, "Gee, this is fun!" Other men are absolutely blatant about their flight and will walk out of a room in the middle of a conversation, or will tell their teen to "just shut up," because they "have heard enough".

Often with teens, the flight response is when they storm out of the room and either slam or lock themselves in the bedroom or walk out the door without saying where they're going. Or, sometimes they don't come home at all. Sounds kind of like dad, huh?

Freeze

The last response to a strong emotion is freeze. Freezing is when you see the dog that you've backed into the corner huddle down and accept that they have to take whatever is coming. They put their head down, their ears lay back against their skull and they often end up

> **The 3 "F" Words**
>
> 1) Fight
>
> 2) Flight
>
> 3) Freeze

relieving themselves on the floor. For people, this looks a little bit different but the principle is the same.

Parents sometimes say that it's difficult to deal with their teens because they never talk. If they do communicate, it's one-word answers like "Yah. No. Kinda. Maybe" or the ever famous, "I dunno".

This is often the teens' response to freezing. They are so bombarded with emotions and feelings that they just stand there like a deer in the headlights.

You'll see the person in "freeze" mode accept that he or she has to take what's coming, so they'll often look at the floor and not say anything. In fact, often they'll tune out. When they're asked for their opinion, they won't know what to say and sometimes won't even know that a question has been asked. Again, they're so emotional that they won't be able to think. This is called "stonewalling". Research would suggest that even most men do this and that unless they can find a way to deal with the emotions they will distance themselves further from the family and the situation.

The aforementioned Dr. John Gottman would say that the person who's in flight or freeze mode is "emotionally flooded". In other words, the emotions are so overwhelming that they just can't deal with it. Their emotional center is incredibly over-charged and they're looking for a way out.

Principle #4: Asking the Golden Question

When you see your teen (or yourself) using one of the "F" words, it should be a strong signal. At these times you have to ask the question "Why?" This is by far the most important question you can ask. And be a grown up here. Don't get defensive and think with contempt (see "Contempt" in chapter 1), "Oh brother. What did I do wrong now?" No offence, but get over it! It's not about you and your ego. It's about your kid and how you're going to build a life-long relationship with them. If your teen displays one of the "F" words, chances are they perceive an attack from you or someone else. Regardless of whether they're right or wrong, consciously or unconsciously, they see their own behaviours as a way to get away from this attack. So where did they get the idea that they're being attacked? That's why you ask "Why?" Figure out what you may have done (or someone else) that has put them in this state. Learn from this and once everybody's emotional center drops down to normal, find out for certain when and how they felt attacked. This is SUCH a beneficial conversation to have. Gottman calls it a "Stress-Reducing Conversation" or a "Repair Attempt". And so with this innate instinct to use the 3 "F"'s to ward off attack, always remember that the behaviours you see in your teen may actually be a result of something you've done.

Summary

- There are two parts of your brain that are very important in dealing with your children. One part deals with the emotion, and the other part deals with logic. Don't forget that the emotion always overrides the logic.

- YOU CANNOT THINK WHEN YOU ARE EMOTIONAL!!! STOP TRYING!!!

- The 3 "F" words are responses to perceived attack. If you or your teen is showing them, ask yourself "Why" and come back to it later with your teen.

Chapter 3: How Do I Calm Things Down in The House?

One predictable fact that we know about teenagers is that there is nothing predictable about them. The chaos that they leave in their wake is sometimes so overwhelming that it leaves us not wanting to even be around them. Many times, parents avoid home like the plague. Why be around something that you have no control over? The truth is, you can't control what happens to them. The only person you can control is yourself. To be able to have an impact on the whole house, sometimes we need to start with ourselves.

As I have said before, the part of the brain that shuts down when we (all of us) get emotional is the thinking part. When your teen gets you mad, you lose focus and are unable to make logical decisions. That's why when our kids fight we come up with brilliant solutions like, "Nobody in this house will touch another person EVER AGAIN! Do you understand me?" Nope. I don't. To be effective in changing the atmosphere in our homes, we have to have the ability to be logical in a storm. We need to find ways of bringing ourselves down when we're feeling extremely emotional.

A lot of people have said to me, "Okay, define EXTREMELY emotional. How extreme is extreme enough?" The answer is, if your heart rate is over one hundred beats per minute (bpm) and you're not doing any physical labor, it's responding to some signal from the emotional center, generally speaking. Now one hundred bpm may sound like a lot because most people's resting heart rate is between sixty to eighty bpm, but it constantly amazes people who are hooked up to a heart monitor in my office how fast they can get to one hundred bpm when they are talking about something that bothers them.

One day, my wife and I got into a fight. It was a good one that ended up with me storming out of the house to go to the gym to try to blow off some steam. The gym is about a ten-minute drive from my house. Once I got to the gym, I signed in, went and put my stuff in the locker, weighed myself, and then walked into the room with the bikes to begin my warm-up. Now, why am I telling you all of this? Is it because I think you really care about my workout routine? No, it's because I want you to get an idea of how long it took me to get to the point where I placed my hands on the heart monitor on the handles of the exercise bike. It had been about twenty minutes or so since I slammed the door to the time that I sat down and started pedaling. As the heart monitor started taking the reading, I noticed something interesting. It kept going up. Finally it beeped to give me my reading and it said that my heart rate was about one hundred and eight beats per minute. Now, I'm not that out of shape that a walk from my car into the gym should put my heart rate at such a high level. What happened was that my body was still reacting to the fight I had twenty minutes earlier. I was still emotional, and in fact, my brain was still not functioning at an optimal level.

John Gottman did some great research about this. He found that when a person's heart rate exceeds one hundred bpm and they try to calm down, normally it will take about thirty minutes for a man's brain to come back to an optimal level. For a woman it takes about twenty minutes…not because they're better, but they're wired differently than a man. So you can expect that you will be brain dead for about thirty minutes AFTER you're in a fight. But, what is it that gets us so ramped up?

Principle #1: Triggers

Each of us as individuals has grown up in our own individual situations. Even siblings have reported that their experiences of their "growing up years" were completely different than those of their brothers or sisters. Each of us has also had unique life experiences and lessons taught to us throughout our lives. Because of this, each of us has what are called "triggers" or things that set us off that are unique. Triggers are events or instances that increase the activity in the emotional center in your brain, because they are connected to your past experiences. They are things that if you see them happen, all of a sudden you're immediately emotional. Do not stop, do not pass go, you're there.

For one person a trigger may be the way a child responds to pain. Another trigger for a parent may be the way that their spouse reacts to them when they are disciplining their child. Another huge one for many couples is when your partner gives you the "look". You know the one. The look that's like a laser beam your partner fires directly at your chest. Bill Cosby describes this look as "Her head split right open, right down the middle and laser beams shot out from her eyes". Usually these triggers can be linked to experiences or values that were imbedded from a very young age.

Part of being a responsible parent is having

Triggers for fathers may include:

- Watching the way a child responds to pain.
- The way that their spouse reacts to them when they are disciplining their child.
- Not feeling like they are being respected.
- A look on a child or spouses' face.
- Being tired.
- Having low blood sugar.
- Having a person cut you off in traffic.
- Fearing for the safety of your child.
- Not being able to provide for the family.
- Loosing or changing jobs.

the understanding of who you are as an individual and knowing why you act the way you do. This is often not an easy process. Triggers can be simple things like being tired, having low blood sugar, having a person cut you off in traffic, etc. Sometimes triggers can be huge, such as fearing for the safety of your child, the stress of money (or lack thereof) or losing or changing jobs. The list is potentially endless.

Sometimes the triggers we have are actually something that has occurred for us in the past and we are just re-experiencing it all over again. It's really important to be able to understand when you are feeling triggered as a parent, and to recognize where it's coming from. Being able to understand the nature of your triggers allows you to better prepare yourself when you get into different situations that may cause anxiety, stress, anger, frustration, fear...you get the point.

Sometimes we're aware of some of those triggers and can list them off quickly. For our other triggers, often we will need to discuss them with people who know us pretty well and get their point of view. If they truly love us and want the best for us, you may be surprised at how well these people know what "sets you off". These people may be you spouse, your best friend, your own parents, maybe a close co-worker, and often even a counsellor or therapist. A good therapist can help you to see who you are in a different light and may actually be able to see things that your family and friends never would. Whoever you choose, it's important to have a fairly detailed understanding of what it is that sets you off. Write these triggers down as a list that you can refer back to when you unexpectedly find yourself feeling one of the "F" words and see if you can track back to what may have set you off.

Putting the Triggers Together

Remember that this list constantly changes so don't think that these are the only triggers you will ever have. If you come across others in the future, come back to the list and add them. Maybe you're able to deal with certain things and specific triggers are no longer valid. Cross them off the list. This is a tool that you can (and hopefully will) use for many years to come.

It's important to understand how triggers interact with each other. Each of them individually may be of significance, but why is it the some days just the smallest of things will set you off and other days it appears that you can handle just about anything?

Principle #2: The Joker Effect

I want to talk about something that I call the "Joker Effect". I'm a movie fan as you've probably noticed and one of my favorite movies is "Batman". I'm talking about the one that starred Michael Keaton as Batman and Jack Nicholson as the Joker. In the movie, the Joker was trying to take over the world (as any good villain should) by putting a toxic chemical into everyday products. The effect was that the person who was poisoned ended up bursting into uncontrollable laughter and died with an exaggerated smile on their face. At first, the community couldn't figure out what the product was that the Joker had tampered with that was killing people. Finally Batman figured out that it wasn't one product in particular. It was a combination of products that had a multiplier effect. Wearing hairspray alone wouldn't kill people, nor if they were wearing only lipstick or deodorant. But the combination of the three was lethal.

I've noticed that people who have a difficult time with their emotions towards their children generally suffer from the same problem. Normally, parents don't go from calm to upset in a heartbeat for no apparent reason. Usually things have been building up during the day and this one thing tends to put it over the top. For instance, if I come home and I'm really tired because I've been in appointments all day, usually this won't cause problems for me. Alternately, if I'm feeling pretty good, but my daughter is whiny, again I can generally handle it. Or if I come home and I'm not overly tired, or my daughter isn't whiny, but my wife tells me that my kids have been really difficult throughout the day, again, generally I'm okay. However, if I come home and I'm tired, my daughter is really whiny, and my wife tells me that my kids have been a real challenge AND my kids are mad because they don't like something we're having for dinner, I have a really hard time controlling my emotions.

The Joker Effect for parents is when you have a combination of different triggers that build up and build up to the point where you're emotional and your limbic system is in overdrive. Again, when I say emotional, that can mean a myriad of different things. That can mean frustration, anger, sadness, grief, fear, disgust, etc. When I speak to parents, often they will say that the most frequent emotion is frustration, but don't be limited to this alone when you're thinking about your interactions with your kids.

I said before that it's really important as parents to understand what our triggers are. There are a couple of reasons for making that statement. Sometimes teens will say to me as I am working with their family that, "Mom and Dad just blow up for no reason". When you speak to the parent, they say that the reason that they get mad is because that the teen did something to make them mad. Sometimes they're absolutely right. Other times, when the parent really explores it, the child did something, yes, but other things triggered the parent, and the behaviour of the child was just the last thing that set them off. It's essential as parents that we know and can recognize the difference. We can't blame our teens for things that aren't their fault in the first place.

The second reason for understanding what our triggers are goes back to the brain structure. That's why I said before that this one principle may be THE most important thing you can learn as a parent. Again, the rule is that if you're emotional or upset, the thinking part of your brain stops working. And yet time after time, parents try to talk "rationally" with an irrational teen, and the whole time their own brains aren't functioning properly because they're upset too. I hear those parents saying things like "my child just won't listen to reason". And we are surprised at this? Of course they aren't going to listen to reason! They can't. It's not that they won't, even though you may think that they're intentionally trying not to listen. The simple fact is that they're too emotional. So what do you do about it?

Principle #3: Soothing the savage beast.

So now that I've told you what to look for, what's next? How do you deal with the fact that you're triggered or upset? Everyone who reads this will have had some point in their lives where they feel sad, scared, frustrated, upset, or whatever you can think of. That's what makes us human. And don't forget, THIS IS NOT A BAD THING. But when you're emotional you can't think. Again, it's a biological fact. So what we have to do is learn how to do something called "self soothing". This is a fancy way of saying that you need to calm down.

Now that you've started to make a list of what your triggers are, you will start to learn beforehand when you're becoming agitated. So as you go through your day, make a mental note of what triggers are happening for you. These will happen for you at work, at home, even as you're driving to and from the places you need to go. As you make these mental notes, check and see how high up on the "Joker Scale" you are. It's like consistently doing a self-evaluation.

As I said before, I'm aware that one of my triggers is being tired from a long day at work. So I've learned a technique that seems to work well for me. At the end of the day when I come home from work, I sit in my car and make a mental note to myself that I'm no longer at work. I turn off my car, put my keys on the seat next to me and then put my hands on the steering wheel. Next, I close my eyes. In my mind, I can see myself taking off my work jacket, and putting on my home jacket. This reminds me that all of the triggers and all of the things that have built up throughout the day need to remain outside of my house.

I've heard other people talk about how they visualize before they go into their house. For some people, it may mean that they visualize sitting on the beach somewhere. When I tell people this, sometimes they think that it sounds a little bit weird. Other people tend to embrace it right away. What ever you believe, just try it. Another thing you may want to try is listening to some calming music. Remember that this is just what works for me. You need to learn what works for you.

Calming down techniques
- STOP – for at least 30 minutes
- Listen to music
- Go for a walk
- Go to the gym
- Play video games
- Take a shower/bath
- Work in the garage
- Meditate
- Coffee/tea
- Watching TV
- Talking to someone
- Prayer
- Etc.

Dealing with your emotions in a healthy way is very simple. It's actually really funny that the way to deal with emotions is often times what parents tell their own children to do. Parents will sometimes tell their children to go to their room, calm down and take a timeout. That's exactly what you need to do when you feel really emotional. Take the time out to calm yourself down and come back to the situation when you're not so emotional. You need to feel safe so you say to your child, "Sweetheart…", or "Buddy…" (or whatever word you choose to use at that moment) "…right now I'm feeling very (insert feeling here). I need to take some time to calm myself down before I can sit down and talk to you about these things." Then walk away and take some time to really relax yourself. You should plan on spending about twenty or thirty minutes doing this. This may seem like you're actually suppressing the emotion, but you're not. You've recognized that you're feeling emotional, and you're doing something about it. You're not necessarily "controlling" your emotions. You're "managing" your emotions. There's a big difference between the two, and allowing your children to see that is very important. They're watching you.

Take a moment and grab a pen and piece of paper **right now**. It has been my experience that when some people read that in books, they just keep reading. If that is you, fine. Don't get a pen and paper. I promise you though that if you can't take that one simple little step, you will not become the parent you want to be. You are taking the time to read this…you might as well take the time to actually do what I am suggesting.

Now that I have laid the guilt down and you have got the pen and paper, write down some of the things you can think of that are calming to you and have helped you relax in the past. In the same vein, think about places you've gone in the past that were really relaxing and can bring back calming memories for you. Write them down. Once you have a list, go through and try to prioritize them. In other words, does working out do more for you than going for a walk? Does listening to music do more for you than just visualization? These are what I call "anti-triggers". When you find the things that are big and have the strongest effect for you, these are the ones that you want to find time to do. If you can do them daily, that's great. If you have stretch it to twice a week, that's okay, but they better be things that REALLY work for you. Don't go more than three days without doing something that reduces your stress and brings you back down to an even keel. I guarantee that if you take fifteen minutes out of every day to do this, your life will improve in many ways, not just how you deal with your kids. How can I guarantee that? I have two words. Coca-Cola.

Principle #4: The Law of the Coca-Cola Bottle

I can honestly say that I think I have drunk way too much Coke in my life. I remember one day when this caused me a real problem. I had just left one meeting, and was racing towards the next one having had no lunch or anything to drink for most of the morning. I reached down and grabbed a bottle of Coke that had been sitting in my hot car since the day before. As I cracked open the bottle, I heard of voice inside my head say "Oh no". The Coke in the bottle had been warmed and the pressure in the bottle exploded everywhere. Both of my arms were soaked in Coke, and it started to run down my suit on to my legs. I had no time to go home and get changed so I had to go to my meeting covered in it. I was absolutely embarrassed. As I sat there in my sticky mess, I had really hard time concentrating on the presentation that I was supposed to be giving. It was the worst meeting I had ever been to in my life. I couldn't think straight, I couldn't remember what I was trying to say, and I think I made really bad impression on the people I was visiting with. The whole time I was focused on how uncomfortable I was sitting in Coke soaked clothes.

So what does that have to do with raising children? I had let the pressure in the Coke bottle grow. I had let it build up and build up without releasing some of it over time. Unfortunately, the results were disastrous. I wasn't able to focus, and I wasn't able to accomplish anything that I wanted to. The same thing can happen with your children. If you have too much pressure in your bottle as you're trying to speak to your children, there's a very good chance that something will explode. It's not because you're doing something wrong or your child's doing something wrong. The fact of the matter is that the part of your brain that's in charge of emotions is simply overriding the part of your brain that thinks.

This principle is not just for dealing with your families either. It applies to all situations where you're forced to use your mind. If you're at work and your bottle is too full of pressure, you won't be able to focus. When you're in a meeting for your church or community organization and you're feeling the emotional pressure of life, you'll probably do or say something that you may not want to. You need to be able to recognize the pressure in your life before you can try to solve any of life's problems. Remember, when you sit down and talk to your child there's a very good chance that you'll become emotional very quickly. Remember the triggers? It's just the nature of the beast. So take the time every day to release some of the pressure out of your bottle. The more often you do this, the less of a chance there is that you will explode when you don't want to. Remember the old adage: "Calmer heads prevail". The funny thing about those old sayings is that there's usually some truth to them.

Principle #5: Being positive about the "negative" emotions

It's important at this point to take a moment to pause and think about the term "negative" emotions. A lot of times people will talk about sadness, anger, fear, and frustration as being negative emotions. Says who? Why are these things considered to be negative? I don't see them as negative at all. I believe that all of the emotions we feel are good. Think about it for second; emotions are naturally a part of us. If we're trying to hide or suppress what we're feeling, we actually add more pressure to our personal bottle and create more turmoil in our life. Another thing that happens when we try to hide or suppress our "negative" emotions is that we're actually modeling behaviour for our children. What that means is that we're teaching our children that they're not allowed the have the emotions that they're feeling when we suppress our own in front of them. We're perpetuating our children's belief that they're not allowed to feel.

I remember a time many years ago when I was at the zoo. There was a new exhibit with beluga whales in a tank with viewing windows underneath so people could see what whales look like in the water. I saw a boy who was probably seven or eight years old running down the stairs towards the tank. You could see the complete excitement in his eyes. Apparently the whales had splashed some water over the top of the tank because the concrete near the bottom was wet. As this boy hit the bottom stair, his foot slipped from underneath him and he went flying. He landed on his hands and knees. After about two seconds he started to absolutely wail. He stood up and both his hands and knees were bleeding. He turned around and looked for one of his parents. I looked up to see his father running down the stairs towards him. When his father got to him, he grabbed him by the arm and yelled at him to stop crying. He told his son that these were just small scratches and that it was nothing to cry about. Now, I'm not a doctor, but from where I was sitting these did not look like small scratches. It looked like something that I would have felt like crying about too. I felt very sorry not only for the boy, but for the father as well.

What this dad didn't realize is that he had just told his son that the "negative" emotions he was expressing weren't appropriate.

Basically, he told his son he wasn't allowed to cry. The lesson that this child likely took from this was that he's not allowed to feel sad or hurt. What a shame that as men we're taught that it's not okay to cry. When you as a parent try to suppress your own feelings, you're showing your child that they can't those feelings either. It's important to learn how to express these "negative" emotions in a healthy way. By doing this yourself, you're teaching your children it is okay to do the same thing when they need to.

Summary

- Really, the only person you can control is yourself. So start there.

- 100 bmp = brain dead.

- Each of us has triggers that are specific to us, that often have nothing to do with the people around us.

- Calm down. You need to take a time out when you can't think.

Chapter 4: What Do My Kids REALLY Need?

Here's an interesting piece of trivia. Did you know that every day the average person in North America is subjected to about 3000 pieces of advertising? Every day! That's about 1,068,000 pieces of advertising every year. Its kind of mind boggling really. Each of these pieces of advertising will tell you how their product is the best, what you can't live without, why you are lonely and depressed (because you don't have their product) and what you need. It gets kind of confusing.

As parents, we're also given a lot of information on what your kids supposedly need from various sources. Our own parents, our in-laws, the guy you work with, experts with leading-edge research whose opinion will probably change next week anyhow…etc. Parents come to me and say, "Jay, I am sick of being told different things from different people. Is there something that's consistently agreed upon across all boards that I can take back to my home today?" In short, yes there is.

Principle #1: The Velcro Theory

Velcro has got to be one of the coolest inventions ever (outside of duct tape of course). The applications are limitless. It can be used for everything from holding together diapers, shoes, bike helmets, and even by those morons who want to see how high they can stick themselves on a wall. There's one annoying thing with Velcro though. If you don't stick it on right or it gets pulled the wrong way and becomes a little bit detached, the little hook things will grab onto anything else that it comes in contact with. You end up either having to fight to get the other things off, or the Velcro un-sticks itself totally and whatever you want stuck gets unstuck. Another problem with Velcro is that the more often you undo the Velcro, the less it sticks.

Nice little story, isn't it? Let me "pull this analogy apart" (excuse the pun) piece by piece and apply it to your teens, your partner, and even you.

Principle #2: Holding it Together from the Beginning

Eddie Murphy starred in a movie with Steve Martin called "Bowfinger" in 1999 that I think about every time I talk about this principle. In this movie, Eddie plays two parts. The first role is that of a paranoid famous actor who believes that aliens are going to come and take him back to a mother ship. He's part of a cult-type organization where they wear Pyramids on their heads. The leader of this group has taken on the role of life coach and has coached Eddie Murphy's character to repeat the phrase "Keep it together, keep it together" over and over when he's panicking. As you learn about this first part of the Velcro Theory, keep in mind the phrase, "Keep it together".

Attachments and Dad

It is often believed that bonding with kids in the early years is mom's territory. Guys are not physically able to have the same kind of bond as the mom so they shouldn't even try. Sorry, but that is plain stupid. Mom has 9 months of bonding during pregnancy, they have opportunities to bond through breast feeding, etc. Absolutely. I agree with that totally. It is an amazing bond that moms can have with their children, BUT THAT DOES NOT PRECLUDE DAD FROM HAVING A SIMILAR BOND. Dads are an important part of the child's life, and the more connections that a child can have, the more secure they will feel in their lives. Children need their fathers to actively participate in their raising and daily care. They need their dads to connect with them and help to fulfill the drive to connect and bond. Individuals and society can no longer afford to use the excuse of "that's mom's territory" because they feel uncomfortable in participation. Your kids *need* you to connect with them. That includes being okay with the snot and tears emotional breakdown because your daughter just broke her favorite sunglasses. It means understanding that they likely don't care that when you were younger you walked over three miles to school in a blizzard barefoot, and you were thankful for the experience. It means not only being in the room, but actually participating in the "sex talk". The list goes on, but they also need you to comfort them when they need it and leave them alone when they need that too.

When we're born, we're programmed to find another surface (person) to stick to. We're driven to do this. In fact, aside from obtaining food, this is probably the strongest desire that we have as humans. Most often this is our mother first, but it doesn't have to be. It's important to understand that the more healthy attachments we make as a newborn the better it is for us. It increases our security, and actually helps to build the brain cells and make connections in our brains that are needed for life.

Attachments occur when children find someone who can respond to their needs and provide physical and emotional nourishment. I'm not going to go into what a young baby needs here because there are hundreds of books that outline these needs in detail. Suffice it to say, the newborn needs to be fed, protected, safe and feel trust for their caregivers, and have some form of reciprocal communication through touch and love and kisses.

Remember that this need to connect is a basic need that lasts for our entire lives. When a young child does not have these needs met, often they're diagnosed with something called "Failure to Thrive". These attachments have such a large impact on a child's growth and development that children who don't find an attachment early in their lives to latch on to won't grow and develop physically, emotionally, and intellectually. This lack of attachment can have life-long impact for them and often shows up later in life as major behavioural and emotional disorders. That's not to say that if your teen has behavioural or emotional problems it's because you as a parent have failed to attach with your child. It's just one of a million sources that we may see negative behaviours coming from.

In a lot of ways, your teens and even you aren't much different from little babies. Again, attachment is a lifelong process. We all want someone we can attach to. Remember that attachment means someone that we know that we are safe with, can be trusted, takes care of us, and participates in reciprocal communication. Believe it or not, your teen really does want to attach to you. You have been there from the beginning, and you have gone through a lot together. Although you can't change the patterns of attachments you've had in the past, you can change where you're going with your teens and the attachment you have to each other from here on out.

Principle #3: How to Make the Velcro Stick

I have this pair of jeans that I have had for years. There are holes in the knees, in the thighs, and one is threatening itself on the backside. As a matter of fact, I can tell exactly how long I have had them because I can match the various tints of paint stains on them to rooms in houses I have lived in. I love them. They're comfortable and provide a nice breeze on hot days because of the holes. My wife on the other hand hates them. When I wear them I get, in the following order, the eye roll, the sigh, and the "You aren't really going to wear those outside of the house, are you?" Yes I am in fact. They're comfortable.

We all like things that are comfortable. We all like to relax and do things that come naturally to us. Often as parents we fall into the trap of being comfortable: "This is the way I have done things for years and I see no reason to change." In some ways, this is akin to the person who says, "There's nothing wrong with me. It's the rest of the world that's screwed up".

Making the Velcro stick takes more than doing things that are comfortable for you. It takes real effort to go outside of what you would normally feel comfortable doing, but recognize that it isn't all about you. It's about how you and your teen connect with each other.

As I said before, attachments can start even before the child is born. With teens, attachment forming takes on a bit of a different format. Playing peek-a-boo with your teen may not be the best way to spend a Saturday afternoon, but just like attachment is for life, the principles behind the ways to create a strong attachment are likewise for life. Really, there are thousands of ways for you to attach with your teen, but here are a few simple ways to get closer to your teen and build those attachments any time. Remember that some of these examples are "Dad friendly", but moms and dads can use all of the following.

Contact

One of the best ways to build a strong attachment with your teen is through touch. Now I understand that some dads really are not touchy-feely so I'm not proposing that you cuddle up on the couch with your 15-year-old son. But you might. It all depends on what you both feel comfortable with. Although you may not be comfortable with something, they might be. The opposite is also true. They may not be comfortable with something you are. You will get your cues from their body language. For instance, if they're trying to get away from you or squirm away, it's a pretty clear sign that they're feeling a bit uncomfortable. Also, be aware that if you have never really given them hugs or cuddled with them, it may be a bit weird for them if you start doing so all of a sudden. "But Jay said this was a great way for us to be closer to each other". You might get some weird looks from your family members. Try hugs, sideways hugs, kisses on the head, neck rubs, arm around the shoulder, tickling, cuddles on the couch…the list goes on. Again, take your cues from your teens. You already probably have a general idea of what they like and don't like so start with that and build from there.

Shared Activities

There is a father that I work with who has a cabin a couple of hours away from his home. On weekends, he takes his daughter up to the cabin and they go on their ATV's to this certain area through the forest. They have done it so many times that they have a special code word to describe what they are doing. Parents who spend time in recreational activities, learning activities like crossword puzzles, board games, or learning the steps to the new dance your daughter is practicing for dance class will automatically increase your connection and attachment.

I had a dad I worked with who has a son who loves fishing. The dad on the other hand found that fishing was the biggest waste of time and could not understand why his son was so passionate about it. But, he went with his son. It didn't matter that he hated the idea of sitting on a little rickety boat at 4 in the morning. He forced himself because he wanted to do things that his son enjoyed. He went outside of his comfort zone.

Dr. Dad

Something that I have noticed over the years as I have worked with dads is that often they will take a back seat to mom when it comes to taking care of the kids if they are sick or having a bad day. Really, how hard it is it guys to make a bowl of soup or to clean out the barf bowl? How difficult is it to sit on the bed next to your teen who has a fever and hold a cold cloth on their head? It isn't. Granted, my wife knows so much more about that medical stuff than I do but that doesn't mean I can't be the go-fer boy. Some of my closest moments with my children have been when they are sick and just want a cuddle with dad. That goes for when they were younger and even now as teens. If you as a parent take the time to do this, your closeness will increase.

Shared Time

Shared time is very different than the activities spoken of above. Activities are physical things that you do together. Shared time is something different. I once worked with a dad who owned his own business and was probably one of the busiest men I've ever met. He had little time for excess. And he absolutely hated rugby. It frustrated him to watch people play a game "where they can't decide if they are playing football or soccer". Even though others disagreed with him, his feelings were pretty strong. His son was one of those people who disagreed with him. His son was actually infatuated with the game. He knew the stats, the players on just about every team…needless to say, his feelings were totally opposite to his father. This dad then did something really amazing in an effort to get closer to his son. He took the time to go onto the internet and find the playing schedule of his son's favorite team. Now, every time the team plays, he makes sure to ask his son how the team did. It's a simple two-minute conversation, but in this one question his dad is saying, "You're important enough to me that I will make an effort to make what you feel passionate about important to me regardless of what's happening for me". As an aside, these guys are best friends. It's really wonderful to see.

Another father I knew grew up with four brothers and no sisters. His first child was a girl. He confided to me, "Jay, I had no idea what to do with a girl. Playing tea party? Give me a break! Nothing exploded or made machine-gun sounds!" He pushed himself to do the "girly things" and actually looked pretty good in a tutu. I remember when it was time for training-bra shopping, he offered to drive with his daughter and her mom. He dutifully sat outside the change room as the girls did their thing. This guy did nothing, but by just being there he let his daughter know that these milestones in her life were important enough to him to spend the time being there.

Identity

Everyone likes to feel that they belong. It is in fact one of the basic needs that we have as humans. We want to know that we fit and are similar to those around us in some way, shape, or form. I've worked with gang members over the years and the one reason why they say they're involved with gangs is because "they're like my family. I belong". Attachment through identity comes from the thought that we are similar to our parents and siblings. We have things in common. Identity can come from a sense of nationalism, race, religious beliefs, work ethic, proximity in living space, etc.

A really simple example, but one that helped a friend of mine to have a sense of identity with his family was that his dad used to say things like, "You're a Robertson and Robertson's don't do that sort of thing". He knew that he was part of a family that had standards and even thought he was very different than his siblings and parents in some ways, he was a Robertson.

"I Matter"

In some ways, this is similar to identity. It's a sense that we belong. Strong attachments occur when we know that we matter to someone else. That means that we spend time and energy becoming involved with our children. This is kind of a tough one for some dads just given our schedules. We have to find ways to separate time for our kids individually, and really be involved with them.

I know father that who has six kids. He works from seven in the morning until about six in the evening just to keep a roof over their heads. This father does two things to let his kids know that they matter to him. First, every Monday night they have a family night. They all get together and play board games, watch a movie together, read scriptures together and have treats. Second, this father has "Daddy Date Night". Every second Friday of the month, he takes one of his kids out to have a special night together. With the younger ones he may go to the park and play on the swings and then out for ice cream. With the older ones, he might go out to dinner, go test-drive cars with his 17 year old son who's mechanically inclined, take his daughter who loves playing the violin to the symphony…in other words he gets creative and does things that they kids would appreciate. They get their "Daddy Date Night" only twice a year given the family dynamic and finances, but when they do it is a big thing. They remember it and will talk about it with whomever will listen.

Principle #5: When the Velcro Doesn't Stick

There are many reasons why these attachments may become stressed. Attachments are for life, but they need to be maintained and worked on. One of the most important issues in teenage life is trying to fit in. I think most everyone can remember the anxiety that came as a teen when we tried to "fit in" to a particular group. The group names may have changed (what was once the "preppy" group has now changed to something else) but the desire to attach themselves does not change. It gives them security in knowing where they fit in socially. When teens are searching to find a social attachment, it often will put a strain on the attachments they have with their parents and family. More often than not, these attachments they develop with their peers will supersede the attachment with their family. In other words, death by being attacked by fire ants would be preferable to going to a movie with your parents when you could been seen by your friends. This is when the Velcro isn't totally attached and it sticks to anything it comes in contact with.

Don't forget that these social attachments are similar for you as well. How many times do we as men do or say things because it's what a man should say or do? How many times do you couch your responses to people in an effort to fit into what's expected, either at home or at work? I think if we're honest, it happens quite a lot. We want to fit into that group because we feel comfortable knowing, "this is me".

What needs to be understood here is that this is natural. Your teens are trying to find their place in the world and it's often independent of you. They don't want to be known as your son or daughter, they want to be known as just them. You can't take it personally because as soon as you do you lose the perspective that your teens are equals, within reason.

I sat in a doctor's office recently and saw a really cute exchange between a little girl who was probably 18 months and her mother and father. In the waiting room there was a table on the opposite side of the room that this little girl really wanted to play with. How do I know she really wanted to play with it? She stood in between her mother's knees and would look at the table, then look up at her mom and dad and take a couple of steps away. Every once in a while she would turn around to make sure that her parents were still there, and then proceed to take a couple of more steps towards the table. On occasion she would turn and run back into the arms of her mom or dad, squealing and laughing as she felt their arms protecting her. Then she would venture out again. It was like there was an invisible elastic band between the girl and her parents. Finally, once she had felt that she was totally safe and that her parents were not going to leave her but be there to protect her if she needed it, she was able to get to the table and explore the objects, bringing them back to her parents when she found something of interest (like a pair of Hanna Montana sunglasses that she put on upside down. Very cute!)

This to me was a great example of coach to caddie, with a strong emphasis on attachment. Even at 18 months, these parents knew that it was their job to let her explore her environment in a way that allowed her opportunity to come back and check in with them when she felt she needed to. Attachment is knowing that the relationship you have with the other party is available to you at all times, and in all places.

Attachment in the teen years is a fine balance between seeking autonomy and wanting to be taken care of. It's the elastic band: stretching and pulling, and then sudden retracting and the need to be close to you.

Simply put, they have to know that you'll be there for them when they need you, and willing to let them go when they don't. You have to be ready to sit down with them and have the tough conversations in a way that makes them think, "Wow! They really listened to me and helped me make the decisions I needed to make". You have to get over the "I don't know what I'm doing" because none of us do. Don't forget…you're faking it and so is every other parent out there. For most men this is a difficult concept to grasp because we generally are not highly trained in effective communication models with teens and we don't like not knowing what we're talking about. Having an effective conversation with your teen will help to strengthen these bonds and will help to keep the Velcro stuck, even in the tough times. In the next chapter we're going to go over how to have a conversation with your teen in a way that is productive and actually brings you both closer.

Summary:

- The Velcro Model states that we are all born with the innate desire to attach. To what and whom is largely determined by what is available to us.

- Attachment is for life. It is not a disease that you outgrow when you hit puberty. Even you have this drive.

- Attachment in the teen years is a fine balance between "Go away!/Please don't leave".

- Comfort is something that we have to overcome when we're trying to connect to our teens. Often the most attachment building moments in our lives with our teens are the ones where we feel uncomfortable and have no idea what we're doing.

- There are a lot of ways to attach to our teens and our teens to us, but the one thing to remember is that it means focusing on their needs first.

Chapter 5: How do I have an effective and meaningful conversation with my teen?

Have you ever asked yourself or others, "Why won't my teens listen to me?" Probably everyone who has ever had a kid has asked that. So what do you think your teens talk about when they come and talk to someone like me? They're asking, "Why won't my parents listen to me?" No big surprise here, but communication is very important in relationships. Modern models of communication actually came from wars. Sociologists wanted to understand effective communication so they looked at how people involved in war were able to get their messages across so effectively. What they noticed was that with radio communication, only one person could talk at a time. So while one person would talk, the other side would listen. When they were done, they would say something like "Over", which signified to the other side that they were done and the other person could talk. That's how the stereotypical "effective listening" models in the 80's and 90's came from where one person would say, "I feel very angry right now" and the other person would say, "I hear that you're feeling angry". This, by the way, has been shown in research to be very ineffective in an emotional discussion because parroting doesn't get down to what is really going on. Nonetheless, this is where effective communication theories came from. To really understand how to be effective in communication, we have to look at it from the back end of things, the listening side, and then we will look at the talking side of things because really the most important part of communication is listening. We have to listen. That means for our teens AND us as parents.

Principle #1: I Feel Like I'm Talking to a Brick Wall!

In some ways, you really are. When people communicate, more often than not, it's through a solid brick wall. This wall represents all of the things that you bring into the conversation. Your perception of the situation, your perception of the other person, your past history with having conversations on this topic, your upbringing, the importance you place on the consequences of the conversation, etc. The other person brings exactly the same thing to their side of the conversation as well. These things become barriers to conversation and can have a huge impact on the outcome.

When we're "discussing things", usually what we're trying to do is to have the other person see our side of the argument. We have a point that makes total sense to us and often the frustration in conversation comes when the other person is so stupid that they can't see what we plainly see. As my wife jokingly says, "You mean the world doesn't see it my way? You're kidding!" Let me give you an example. Let's say your twelve-year-old son tells you that he wants to go to a party where the other kid's parents are out of town and you know that there will be drugs there. The conversation may look like this;

Son: Yah, but dad, everyone is going! And really, the only drug that will be there is pot, and that really isn't that bad.

You: Look, drugs are drugs. On top of that, this kid's parents aren't even going to be home. This just has bad news written all over it. You're too young to be doing drugs.

Son: Give me a break! How old were you when you got stoned for the first time? Twenty? This isn't the seventies anymore dad. Everyone does drugs. It isn't a big deal.

You: Look, you are not going. Period.

Son: Oh sure. I'll just give up the chance to go to this party because my daddy said I should. That'll make for a great conversation with my friends.

In this conversation, can you hear both sides of the argument? Let's look at it from the son's point of view first. Everything about being a teenager is focused on being an individual, but fitting into the crowd. There's an old saying that the nail that sticks out is the one that gets hit by the hammer. I remember being twelve (unfortunately). If my parents said I couldn't do something and I had to tell my friends why…yikes! If he didn't go, first of all he would have to explain why to his friends. Second, he would stick out because he wasn't using drugs.

The dad's side may be a little bit easier to see. Regardless of how you personally feel about pot, the dad here felt that twelve was too young to start using. His concern was for what effect this was going to have on his son, and the trouble that may come from being at a party with no adults around.

So how do we deal with this barrier of both sides having a point of view that makes sense to them, but not to the other person? "Just tell them no. I'm the parent and they need to listen". It's an attitude that we as dads sometimes take, but as we've discussed before, this probably won't work out very well for you. I'm constantly blown away by parents who think that they can muscle their kids into compliance. It doesn't work. But something has to give to come to a solution to the problem, so who goes first?

Parents often feel like it's not their job to come around to that other side because, "I'm the parent. I don't need to see their point of view. They should just listen to me". Again, how's that working for you? Probably not very well. It goes back to the "coach and caddie". This may have been how you've dealt with your teens in the past, but unfortunately it's not going to work any more. Really, this attitude of "They should listen to me first" is a bit childish. It's like the little kid who stands in the corner and pouts because they're not the center of attention. "Fine! Then I won't listen!" It's not an effective way of communication. Can you imagine doing that at work? If you wouldn't do it there, you shouldn't do it at home either.

Principle #2: Effective Listening

What I'm about to say is not rocket science. In fact, I would be surprised if you haven't heard most of it before. So why do I choose to include it and waste your time by repeating something you've already heard? I truly believe that there are times that we learn concepts that are critical to our life, and once we get back into living that life, old habits tend to take over. It takes real effort to change your patterns and behaviours. If you stop reminding yourself what you can become, you will continue to be who you are.

In saying that, there really are 3 important aspects of listening. They are:

1) **Don't Listen to Them.**

2) **Respect and Reflect Feelings**

3) **So What Are You Going to Do About It?**

Don't Listen to Them

Sound good? It's easy. To have great communication with your teens, don't listen to them. Here's what I mean. I've found in life that there's a difference between listening and hearing someone. Listening means that you're aware of the information. Period. Hearing on the other hand means that you take in the information, internalize it, and then actually do something about it. So don't listen to your teens. Hear them.

Hearing as opposed to listening takes concentration. True confession. I was playing on my Xbox one night and I was in the middle of a great battle. We were absolutely destroying the other team and my son came home from Scouts. He came downstairs and I was sitting with my headset on talking to the other guys on my team saying things like, "He's up on the ridge on the left" and "watch out behind you!" I was really into this game and we were doing really well. At this point, my son came down and he sat down onto the couch next to me. I said to him, "You really need to get ready for bed. It's past your bed time." He said, "I know dad. I just have a real headache". I was so engrossed in my game that all he got out of me is an, "uh-huh, uh-huh". He kept trying to engage me in this conversation by continuing, "Yah. I was at Scouts and we were playing a game and this kid tripped me and slammed me into a brick wall". "Uh-huh". Unfortunately, I was so involved in what I was doing that I was missing an opportunity to build a relationship with my son and show a little compassion. My wife finally came down and gave me "the look", so I quickly ended the game and went in to see him. He had a really big lump on his head and he was in tears he was in so much pain. My son doesn't generally complain about something unless it's really bad.

Research shows that one of the best tools parents can use in creating positive bonds with their children and teens is to show compassion and empathy when they're hurt, physically or emotionally. This means that we have to do two things: we have to pay attention and then avoid saying something intelligent like "You'll be fine. Stop crying!" When I finally got over myself, I realized that my son really needed me and I was too busy to pay attention. I was listening (actually, I was aware that he was speaking...kind of), but I missed an opportunity to deepen my relationship with my son and really hear him.

To hear fully, you need to need to turn off all of the distractions. Put down the paper, turn off the computer or TV, turn off your phone...you get the picture. If the phone rings, leave it. That's why they invented voice mail. I mean, seriously! Your kid's trying to talk to you! Take it and grab a hold of it like a bulldog on a steak. It may not happen again for a while.

Once you have turned everything off, pay attention. This includes body language. As counsellors, we get into what we call the "counsellor crouch". This means our body is turned towards the person we're talking to, we uncross our arms and legs, we lean forward, and we look the person in the eye. There's nothing more disconcerting than when you're talking to someone and they're turned away, looking around the room, checking out their watch, flicking a pen around, etc. This is saying to the other person, "I really have other things I could be doing right now and what you're saying is kind of boring for me." Your teens will eventually follow your lead in paying attention, but you first need to model the behaviour for them.

Paying attention also means that you need to be quiet. When I say this to many parents, the response I get is, "I AM quiet and I let them talk". It amazes me that when I then talk to the teens of these same parents, they say the opposite; they complain that their parents never let them talk. Let me use an example. Imagine that your car has a bit of a problem and you need to take it into the mechanic. As you walk in the door, the mechanic gives you a smile and says, "How can I help you?" You say, "My car needs some work". At this point, does the mechanic say, "Okay, thank you. The problem is with your fuel intake and the carburetor. I know exactly how to fix it. Leave it here and I will fix it in about an hour and it will be $450." NO! Of course they don't say that. You haven't told them anything. They have no idea what's wrong with the car, so how can they tell you that they know exactly what's wrong, they'll have it fixed in an hour and what the cost is? They can't. The mechanic would say, "So tell me about what's going on for your car. What does it sound like? Have you noticed it when you are idling or when you are accelerating"... etc. When I say that as parents we need to be quiet, this is exactly what I'm talking about. Our kid comes in the door and says, "I've had a bad day today" and in our infinite wisdom as parents we come up with something like, "Well, we all have bad days. Welcome to the real world". And then we wonder why when we sit at the dinner table and say to our teens, "So how was your day?" we get a "Fine". "Anything happen?" "Nope". "What happened at school?" "Nothing". Let me tell you, I would be giving one word answers too if I knew that the person I was going to be talking to was going to "fix my problem" before they knew what it was. BE QUIET! Your kid's talking to you and you do NOT need to solve the problem for them.

Respect and Reflect Feelings

Let's be honest with each other. Even as parents, we have a really tough time trying to balance all of the things that we have to do. Work, parenting, budgeting, in-laws, home renovations, and the list goes on. However, probably the most emotionally intense extended period of our lives is when we're teenagers as you probably well remember. The hormones, the "who is talking about who behind who's back", the acne, which crowd are you in or not in, etc. Frankly, it was the worst time of my life. I was so frustrated and emotional. Now, remember the brain picture that we discussed in chapter 2? The part that's missing for your children also contains part of language that's used when expressing emotions. Your teens very often will not have the words to express their sometimes very emotional world. They can't just sit down with you and say, "Today I was hyper-aroused when Stacey looked at me that way, so I noticed a deep and intense fear which gradually grew into a depressed and heart-rending emotional state." What they will do is come in the house and slam themselves down on the couch and say, "UHHHHHGGGHH! I am just so…UHHHHGGGGHH!" A lot of the time, they don't have the words. They just have a feeling and they know that they don't like it. Part of our job is to help them with the words. Give them some emotional words, but don't tell them what they're feeling. It's a bit of a fine balance here. It kind of goes back to the desire that we have as fathers to try to solve the problem right away. We just want the problem to be fixed so we can move on. What we don't understand is that often our interpretation of the situation may be wrong from their perspective. Let me give you a couple of examples.

Let's assume that your daughter comes home from school and she's crying. You ask her what's wrong, and if she was open enough to you she might tell you, "My life sucks!" When you ask for clarification you get a story about how "Susan said that Mike saw James at the park, and he thought that Amy was talking about my boyfriend who I've been going out for two whole weeks and he's the best thing that ever happened to me, and she was all like, 'Uhhh' you know? How could I even think about showing my face at school now? I wish I could just go into some corner and just die. Nobody would care". Finally she takes a breath and looks at you expectantly. For dads, this is a very scary moment because all of a sudden it's show time. You're on. In your mind you're probably as confused as heck, but as a dad you're supposed to have all the answers, so you had better come up with something quick dad because that's your job after all. It's not true, but often it's the conversation we as fathers have in our brains. Our society has given men the nametag of "problem solver" and so we jump to try to fix it. NOW! This is not necessarily a father's disease however.

When They Don't Open Up

Many times parents will say to me, "I would be happy if my teen would say ANYTHING to me, let alone tell me about how they are feeling. I completely agree. This can be very frustrating. Understand that there are basically 2 reasons why teens may not open up to you. The first reason is that they are trying to be independent and don't want to have to rely on "Mommy" and "Daddy" anymore. They are trying to figure it out on their own. The second reason that they may not open up is because it takes a lot of courage to open up and share feelings...for ANYONE. When you do, you run the risk of not being supported, not being taken seriously, or being misunderstood. The solution to both of these situations is the same. Give them the opportunity to talk over and over again. "You look really upset. Do you want to talk?" If the answer is "no", then leave it alone. Don't berate them and get upset at them because that will only drive them further away (remember the distancing cascade?). And for heaven's sake, don't take it personally. Keep the doors open all the time and eventually they will walk through.

Parents of all types sometimes fool themselves into believing that they're supposed to have all the answers. If they do, they're much smarter than I am!

I've actually seen this situation play out with a friend of mine and watched him try to deal with it. He sputtered, got frustrated, made fun of her a little bit, and then told her, "Don't worry. In a few years when you graduate you won't even associate with these people anyhow." What followed was a screaming tirade with "you never listen to me anyway" punctuated with doors slamming and lots of yelling.

I want to pick apart what may have been going on for my friend, because I think it is a very typical response from a lot of parents to situations like this. The first thing he did was he sputtered. In short, the thinking part of his brain shut down as the emotions he was feeling settled in. He realized that he had no idea what was going on and how can you fully solve a problem that you don't understand? This is when he got frustrated because he knew he was trapped. He had no idea what the problems was and he felt like he was being asked to solve it. Going back to the three "F" words, his response to a perceived attack on his role as an all-knowing parent, was that he responded with an attack back. He made fun of her. Contempt. He turned to me and said, "Is she speaking English? Sometimes she just comes in here and starts flapping her gums like she's trying to say something but the only thing I hear is blah, blah, me, me, wah, wah." Then he came up with the solution. "Don't worry about it". WOW! Profound!

What he hadn't done is taken the time to really hear what she was saying. Buried in that breathless story of a teenage girl are all of the dynamics that are involved in the life of a teenager that you'll probably never fully understand because frankly, neither does she. Instead of trying to fix the situation, stand back and try to realize that you *don't have to fix it*. That's not your job. You're not the coach here. You're the caddie. You just have to get them to take a look around, see the green and ask them, "So how are you going to get there?"

Let's say you're at work and one of your co-workers comes to you and says, "So, I just got out of a meeting with our supervisor and he was saying that Mike in accounting overheard someone talking about how I came in late the other day. He wanted to know if I'm planning on making a habit of coming in late. I can't believe him! What a complete (*fill in the blanks here*)!" How would you respond? You probably wouldn't say something like, "Well, you do come in late sometimes. Maybe you should just show up on time or quit". Even if he did come in late every other day, I can imagine that most people would say something like, "Really? That sucks! That would really make me upset if Mike did that to me. What are you going to do?"

There you have it, the solution to all your problems. In that one phrase, you've actually encapsulated exactly what your teen needs/wants to hear when they talk about their lives to you. Let's go back to your daughter. When she spewed out the rant about somebody named James talking to someone else, imagine inserting the phrase you would have said to your co-worker. Instead of saying, "Well, in three years you won't know them anyway, so get over it", imagine you said, "Really? That sucks! I bet you're pretty mad/frustrated/upset.

What do you think you're going to do about it?" You've identified that they're upset, found a word or two that describes what they may be feeling, you've empathized with them, and then you have given them the respect that you believe that they can come up with a suitable solution. Try to relate to what you're hearing, even if you don't understand the dynamics of a teenage girl's mind. Not in a "you think that is bad, when I was a teen I had something way worse happen" kind of a way. Pick apart what she has just said to you. She sounds hurt, something about her boyfriend, and miscommunication from someone. Now you have something to work with, and you haven't solved a thing!

If this is such an easy process on paper, why is it that parents keep coming to me saying that they can't do that with their teens? It goes back to the glasses you have on in regards to your teen. Or any loved one for that matter. When emotions get involved, we lose perspective. Remember? You lose your brain when you're emotional. In the glasses that we see our teens through, often we will see them as powerless, fragile, and unable to protect themselves. They haven't done a very good job so far, so what makes them or us think they will start now, right? The problem with that thinking is, as I said before, if you keep the padding around them, when are they going to experience life?

Let me give another example. A father and his son came to see me and they were talking about how the son and his mother were always fighting with each other. The son said, "I hate her because she's always telling me what to do". The father responded by saying, "Well, she's your mother so you need to listen to her. And don't say you hate her because you don't. You're just mad at her because you're too lazy to do what you're supposed to do." What do you hear in the father's response? He was dismissive, didn't really hear what the son was saying, and he used contempt. "I say, you do, because I'm the boss". Dad listened, but he didn't hear. What he didn't hear the boy saying was that he was frustrated. Did the son hate his mom? No, of course not but he was upset that his freedoms were being limited and he didn't know how to say it because he didn't really have the language to do it effectively. When the father was coached on what to say, the conversation went as follows:

Son: I hate her because she is always telling me what to do

Father: You sound pretty mad. What sort of things is she telling you to do that makes you feel like you hate her?

Son: Well, like the other day I was up in my room and I was doing my homework like she told me to, then she yelled up to me that I had to come down to clean up from my snack. So I came down and did that and then she told me to go and get my laundry because she was doing a load and when I brought it down, she asked if I had finished my homework, and I said I hadn't. Then she freaked out on me because she said I was screwing around.

Father: So you were really frustrated that she was asking you to do a bunch of things at once and she got mad at you for doing what you were told.

Son: Totally. She does that all the time. I hate her.

Father: Yah, I think I would feel frustrated too. I bet I would also feel confused about what she wanted me to do. Do you feel confused sometimes?

Son: I never know what I'm going to get in trouble for so it's like, I just don't even want to be around her.

What's the difference here? First of all, dad didn't get defensive about the kind of language that the son chose to use about mom. I think that's important because often times we go to a place of "nobody, especially my kids should talk like that about my partner". Yes, but recognize that the child may just not have the language to express how they're really feeling about what's going on, so they may use words that they may not choose to if they had an alternative. The second difference is that dad really tried to listen and see if he could hear what was behind the statement of "I hate her". He asked clarifying questions and was able to relate to the son by saying, "Yah, that would frustrate me too".

It takes time and a lot of effort initially to be able to have a conversation with your child like I have outlined above. You need to put your emotions aside and try to look for what's happening, and then reflect that you're hearing how difficult this is for them. But you don't need to try to solve the problem! Don't even try because it will most likely blow up in your face. Don't just listen to them, instead hear them, respect their feelings, and then ask, "So what are you going to do about it"?

So What Are You Going to Do About It?

I have spent many years in the corporate world and government organizations, and one thing I have come to realize about people meeting together to solve a problem is that there are some good meetings, some bad meetings, and then there are train wreck meetings. In the really bad meetings, there seems to be this underlying current of "I'm smarter than you and you need to do what I say". Some people may argue that this is no longer the feeling in the business world…that we have progressed. Books and lecturers that talk about "Win/Win vs. Lose/Lose" have changed how we view interactions in the business world. Hey, maybe I'm wrong but it has been my experience that in the real world, many people like power and like to let others know they have it.

Let's set a scene to give you an idea of what I'm talking about. I was in a meeting once with various managers from a chain of restaurants. The Area Manager named Bob was in charge of the meeting and he and I were trying to get some ideas of how we were going to market a new product. Bob and I already had an idea of what we wanted, but I convinced him that he should at least ask the managers in case they had any other ideas that we might have missed. When the meeting started we were all sitting around a table and Bob said, "Okay, I already have an idea in my head about how to do this, but I want to hear what you think. So hit me". One of the more vocal managers made a suggestion about doing a radio spot and having the station come on a Saturday night to do a promo. Bob responded, "Do you have any idea how much that would cost? We have a budget that we need to follow here". Another manager said, "What about doing mail-outs?" This was shot down because the demographic we were trying to target was huge in that city and "simple mail-outs" wouldn't hit enough of them with the budget we had. I think there were probably two or three more suggestions that were met with the same response from Bob and then everyone was silent. These people around the table were intelligent individuals who knew the product and believed that it was a great seller, but not one of them spoke up with any more ideas.

After the twenty-minute meeting that was scheduled for one and a half hours, Bob and I left and he grumbled to me "Well that was a waste of time. I can't believe none of them could come up with an intelligent idea." What had happened? It wasn't that they couldn't come up with an idea. It was the way that the ideas were received that caused them to stop trying. What Bob didn't realize was that by placing an immediate judgment on their ideas, he was stifling the ideas that grow from other ideas. What I mean is that everyone in the room became worried that if they put themselves out there with an idea, it would be shot down and they would feel like an idiot in front of others. But what does this have to do with your teens?

When you and your teen have had a conversation where you've paid attention to them and helped them understand the feelings they have about the situation, they're probably going to want to know what to do. So what do you do? If you were their coach you would say, "Well, what you should do is this, that, and then do this as well." As we have discussed before, telling a teen what to do very seldom works the way you want it to. More often than not it will blow up in your face and you will get the "You never listen to me" lecture from them. Remember that your job as a caddie is to stand back and let them play the game. Our job is to ask them, "So what are you going to do about it? What do you think?"

I need you to understand something here. When you ask, "what do you think?" you need to be prepared to hear what they think. I promise you that you will not like some of the answers they give you. "I think I should go to this guy's house to watch movies even though his parents aren't home and we will be all alone on a sofa in a dark room together." AHHHHH! Your initial reaction will be, "I don't think so!" Choke it back momentarily because you can imagine the scene that would follow.

I once knew a dad who was a master at this. You could see the fear in his eyes as his daughter described her desire to try and attract the attention of a new guy in the school. Her original solution to getting his attention was to wear a really "cute" outfit. You can imagine what it looked like. Dad choked back his "where are the rest of the clothes that go with that outfit?" He said, "Okay. That's an option. What else?" The key to what he did was to not evaluate it. Really, it IS an option. But if he had been like the Area Manager Bob, he would have shot it down and said, "No. That's a bad idea". Eventually they will clam up when you do this. Not a good thing.

When you're speaking with your teen about what they should do, pull out a piece of paper and pen and write down all of the options that are available WITHOUT JUDGEMENT! Just put them down. Remember, brain vomiting is a good thing. I have learned that sometimes the stupidest ideas often are the kindling for an amazing idea, so reserve the judgment. Feel free to offer suggestions to the options list, but be ready to have your teen try to shoot it down right away. Don't get frustrated. Let them know that this is a list of possibilities, not a list of "have to do's".

When you have created the list together, what do you do with it? Let me clarify…what do THEY do with it? Remember, this isn't your problem to solve. You're just helping them to see where they're going. But they need to decide how to get there.

Principle #3: Cost Benefit Analysis (CBA)

Anyone who has taken a business course knows the value of cost-benefit analysis. It means taking an option that you have and looking at all of the positives and negatives that can come from a decision. This is without a doubt one of the best tools that I've ever found to help a teen who's trying to make a decision. In a CBA, you take all of the options that you have written down (it has to be written down because it becomes tangible then) in front of you and then take a separate sheet for each of the options and split it down on the middle. On one side of the paper you ask, "What are the positives to this option?" and on the other side you ask, "What are the potential problems with this option". And when I say, "You ask" what I mean is that you let your teen come up with the pros and cons.

I used this tool once with my son with in a situation that may happen to you. My son had an important decision to make. He knew what he wanted to do and so when we got to creating the CBA for his option of choice, the entire side of the pros was full with justifications that were absolutely ridiculous. The con's side on the other hand had two or three possibilities that were pretty watered down. He knew what he wanted to do and he was going to come up with every possible reason why I should listen and agree with him. I want to highlight something about that last sentence. He was going to come up with every possible reason why *I* should listen and agree with him. I learned an important lesson when I saw this list because as I said, he had already made the decision. He knew what he wanted and he thought I was going to say no to him. He was waiting for me to be his coach. I think he got a bit of a shock when I said to him, "Well, looks like you have put a lot of thought into this. Give it a couple of days and keep thinking about it in case you missed anything. I hope it works out the way you want it to." That last phrase wasn't a threat. I really did hope it worked out the way he had envisioned. In the end, he did what he wanted and lived with the consequences. I think if he was faced with the decision again, he may have added a few more cons and been a bit more realistic about the pros, but I gave him the ability to say, "I can make a decision on my own." What an amazing gift to give to your child. To know that you trust them. This is actually one of the fundamental needs that we have as humans: to feel that we are trusted and valued. Does this sound familiar? It is one of the principles surrounding maintaining and developing a secure attachment. Interesting huh? Something to think about.

Principle #4: When the Bad Goes Really Bad

Everything that I've said up to this point in this chapter, and in fact this whole book has been said under the assumption that your teen has some semblance of respect for you. I've been doing this long enough to know that the picture I have painted in this chapter will not always remove all of the challenges you will face as a parent. I've been in rooms where teens have yelled, screamed, and even physically threatened their parents and needed to be restrained. I've also been in the room when teens have told their parents at fourteen that they feel they're ready to be a parent themselves, and are actively seeking a partner to help them accomplish this and nothing mom and dad can do will stop them. All of these situations are scary. My heart breaks for these parents. Being a parent is tough enough without having to sit back and ask, "What am I going to do about a situation where I know that my child is not only in danger, but could actually kill themselves?"

Although this book is not the place to go in depth as to how to deal with severe behavioural challenges or mental health concerns, a couple of thoughts have come to my mind over the years as I have worked with these families. I'm sorry to say that none of these thoughts are "solutions" because one thing that we have been given as humans that is both a blessing and a curse is our agency. Your teens are free to do what they will.

This will be a bit of a rant so I ask for your forgiveness as I do this, but I feel it's important to speak about here. Unfortunately our laws are constantly changing giving parents less control and young children more power than they know what to do with. It is a concern to me to see thirteen year olds given the right to decide if they want to receive medical and mental health treatment. Of course there are some limits to this, but these are pretty important decisions that we are handing over to them. Think about it...the thinking part of the brain has just started to develop in these kids and we as parents are told that they are old enough to make life-altering choices? I don't think so. I would call on the law makers and the leaders of our communities and countries to really take a hard look at what they are doing to our kids by giving the awesome decision making powers. They don't have the ability to handle it.

A lot of times the decisions they make are going to change their (and your) lives, but they need to make them. As parents we could lock them up in their rooms, but again, what would this solve? It would be a temporary solution to a problem that will build as you continue to restrict their movement.

The other thought that I have had surrounds professional help. There comes a time when you can't do it on your own. You need to seek help. There are many good counsellors, therapists, doctors, and social workers out there that have the skills and training to help you learn how to deal with the really tough situations. You can go to my website at www.jaytimms.com and check out how you can contact me directly. Again, your teen has the right to decide whether or not they will go, but if nothing else, you can find the help for your individual situation through these people.

Having said all of that, I'm confident that regardless of the situation you find yourself in with your teen, the principles that I've presented and continue to present here will always have a positive impact on your relationships with your children. You're finding ways to strengthen the relationship between you and your teen. What could be more valuable, even if it doesn't totally "fix" the problem?

Summary

- There may be a reason your teen isn't listening to you. It might be you.

- Stop listening to them. Hear them.

- Have them look for the green and then ask them how they are going to get there by exploring the options with them.

Chapter 6: How Do I Effectively Discipline My Teenager?

So, here's the deal. I know, without a doubt, that some parents will pick up this book, read the chapter headings on the contents page, see this chapter and immediately flip to this part of the book, looking for "the answer". If you're one of those people, I need to explain something. You're not going to get it. Period. Do me a favor. Either buy the book and start the beginning, or put the book back on the shelf where you found it. The point is that parents who are looking to discipline and control their teens above all else are 100%, totally, and completely going to fail at having a great relationship with their teens. I guarantee it. When I do workshops on the topic of raising teens, I always skip this part because there's no way in two hours I can effectively talk about what discipline means and how to do it in a way that actually strengthens the relationship. So, if you've just flipped to this page, do us both a favor and go buy this book or go back to the beginning. However, if you've been following along up until this point, you will understand that discipline is all in how you approach it.

Principle #1: What Works and What Doesn't

I've said up to this point that as parents, we really need to be aware that our teens have the ability to make decisions on their own, so trying to force them or stop them is going to blow up in your face. In general I believe this, but there are times when we as parents need to step in and correct behaviour. Regardless of how old our children become, our responsibility of being a parent never really ends.

In working with parents and families for as long as I have, I've discovered some really great ways to say "no". What I'm not going to do is sit here and tell you step by step the techniques of getting teens to listen. Sorry. I know that will frustrate some people, but let me explain why I'm not going to do that, and what I will do.

When I was doing some research with fathers, I mentioned that I was going to take the information I learned and use some of it to write an instruction manual for dads on how to raise their kids. One of the dads made a really astute comment that has impacted the way that I work with families. He said, "How can you write an instruction manual for teens in general? Each of my kids are so different that if you wrote a book, it would have to have different volumes for each of the kids I have". How true. As I said before, my dad helped me to understand to raise Jay Timms, but I don't have Jay Timms as a child. I have totally different kids.

For me to sit here and tell you specific techniques to use with your child, I would be assuming that your teen isn't unique or individual. I would be assuming that they're like gingerbread men who are all cut from the same mold. So I'm not going to do it.

Here's what I'm going to do though. I'm going to take some time to describe some philosophies or trends that I've discovered in parenting teens. It will be your job to take this knowledge and put it to use with your amazingly unique teen. Remember that none of us know what we're doing anyhow, so you'll have to experiment a bit to find what works for your little hormonal monster. At the end of the day, don't forget that our goal is to find a way to have a meaningful relationship with our teens that is equally satisfying for you and them. It's all about the relationship.

Principle #2: Boot Camp

Boot camp is the most familiar philosophy with most parents. It screams testosterone and is one of the few socially acceptable reactions for dads to their teen's negative behaviours. I have to be honest here. I love getting phone calls from parents who say that their teens are so bad that they need to be "sent off to boot camp or something". I've had a surprising number of these calls over the years. What is as surprising is that some parents believe that if someone else squishes their teen into a hole and forces them to conform that the teen will "see the light" and will remain that way when they come home. I hate to break it to you, but they probably won't."

Boot camps are this wonderful invention that have been immortalized in movies where teens are shipped off and are met by some loud and aggressive adult named "Sir" who puts them through various forms of physical and verbal punishment. At the end of it all, the teen has been "broken" like some wild stallion and comes home understanding themselves a little better and has a deeper understanding and love for their parents. What isn't shown in these movies is what happens 3-4 weeks after the teen has come home. They don't respect the parents any more, there are no harps playing, and there is no peace in the home. Why? Because it doesn't work! Plain and simple. Oh, sure in the short term it may work, but very quickly the teen and the family moves back into our old habits. All of these groups and camps may have great principles and good intentions, but I have yet to see one that truly transforms a teenager into something that lasts for more than a couple of months.

Think about it for a second. When has forceful discipline ever worked? This applies in both the family and on the world stage. When has there ever been a time where one individual or group came into a situation, laid down the law, intimidated people with their awesome power, and then left the situation with a great and positive relationship with the other party? I'm no historian but I can't think of how it would be possible. Go back to the Donkeys-R-Us principle. It's our natural instinct as humans to fight back against people who are trying to force us to do something. Our teens are not being rude, stubborn, or disrespectful when they fight back. It's a natural instinct that even you have. They're fighting against someone who's trying to force them against their will. Oh sure, they may comply for a while but the relationship isn't something that's lasting and positive. It forces your teen into this black hole of fear that often they feel they have no way of getting out of. A lot of times, I see dads fall into this role of commander-in-chief. It's like it's part of our genetic make-up to try to force our children into doing something. I've never seen a positive relationship come from this type of interaction with parent and teen.

In boot-camp discipline, parents will try to tactics of "taking away". Taking away the TV, the video games, the cell phone, social interaction...the list goes on. "Because you did this, you are grounded." Often times I've seen grounding have an indefinite amount of time attached to it. I remember meeting a teen once who said that he was grounded from playing his video games. I asked him how long he was grounded for and he couldn't remember. "Mom didn't really say". In questioning mom, she said that she hadn't given him a limit because it would be given back if he was "good". That word has got to be the dumbest word in the English language. What the heck does it mean to be "good"? This mom had no definition. "He knows what it means", to which he shrugged his shoulders and looked at me like he was saying, "I have no idea". I believed him. As an aside, neither this kid nor his mom could remember why the Game Boy had been taken away in the first place.

So why is boot camp parenting such a widely used form of discipline? The main reason that I have found is because it feels good. Really, really good sometimes. Think about it. You have someone standing in front of you who is absolutely refusing to see logic and is blindly doing something that you know is stupid just to piss you off. It feels GREAT to take a deep breath and let all the frustration come out. And sometimes it works for a while. But only for a while.

R.E.S.P.E.C.T.

Another big reason that dads use this form of intervention is because they want some respect. "My teen doesn't respect me or my rules and so I'm going to do this because it will make them show respect."

Movie time again. In 2008, Iron Man came into theatres. There is one scene where the main character is demonstrating a new weapon to the US Military somewhere in Afghanistan. In his sales pitch he says,

"Some have asked, 'Is it better to be feared or respected'? I humbly ask, 'Is it too much to ask for both?'"

My response to that…it's impossible for both to co-exist. If you don't want someone to think for themselves, learn and grow in life, and have a voice, fear is a great tool. If you want someone to grow and develop, to move ahead and be something, then you have to build a relationship with that someone that will be deep and will last through tough times. There's a distinct difference between respect and fear that I think many parents confuse. Fear is easy to understand, but respect is something totally different.

Respect is a deep emotional MUTUAL connection to someone who you know is there to support you and help you out. It's something that is build over time and can never be forced. "My kids should respect me because I'm the parent". That would be nice wouldn't it? The thing is that I've worked with many parents who really don't deserve the respect that they so badly desire because they haven't worked to build it. It doesn't just happen because you donated some sperm or carried them in the womb for 9 months. Sorry. Respect is something that you feel for someone who has strength of character and someone you aspire to be. I've sat down with many parents who tell me, "You know, when I was a kid I NEVER would have spoken to my mom or dad the way my kids talk to me. If I did, I would have gotten the beating of my life. I did what I was told and I had respect for them." Hey, I may be wrong here, but I can't see how that's possible. They didn't respect them. They feared them. There's a huge difference. These types of relationships often lack depth and emotional connection.

I want to refer back to the issue of attachment, or the Velcro. Attachment comes from a mutual relationship of security, compassion, sameness, and learning about and fulfilling each other's needs. One of the biggest destroyers of that Velcro bond is the contempt that Dr. Gottman spoke of. Remember that contempt is an attitude of superiority that states, "I say, you do". It automatically forces the other person into a position where they try to get away from that attitude. If we're trying to build relationships with our teens, this probably is the wrong way to go about it.

There are many reasons why some people confuse "respect" with "fear", but that's a whole other book that I won't go into right now. Suffice it to say, parents are often so frustrated with their teens that they will do almost anything to make their teens be quiet and listen.

That is one strength of Boot Camp style parenting. If you can scare them into submission, at least they are submissive. I just wonder how long that will last for you?

Boot Camp Traps

Here's a trap that I want you to be aware of if you are raising your teen with a partner that can be really destructive to your relationship with your teen and your partner at the same time. I often see families where one parent (often the dad) is absolutely rigid in the setting rules and the other person (usually mom) will give in sometimes and other times won't. I'm not being sexist here. It's just what I've seen. So once mom gives in, dad figures that he needs to keep tighter "rules" because mom is too giving, so he becomes militant with the rules and so mom gives in a little more because she feels sorry for the teen, and it just spirals. At the same time, the teens are in the middle trying to figure out where the boundaries are and are either confused and scared because they don't know where they stand (think of the middle line on the road) or they get really good at knowing that if I want this, I should go ask dad, but if I want that I should go ask mom. Don't deny it. Your teens are no dummies. Even if it's planned out, this type of "good cop/bad cop" rarely works. It actually drives a wedge between you and your partner, and shows disrespect to the relationship between your partner and the teen.

If you're dealing with this trap, although this is ALSO a topic for another book, let me give you a thought. The relationships you form with your children are precious, but so are the ones with your partner. A lot of what I'm going to present in this book can actually be used in learning how to strengthen the relationship with your partner. Re-read this and instead of reading the words "teen" and "kid", insert "partner", "wife", or whatever your situation may be. Also, raising children can be the most straining thing on an intimate relationship. Be a man. Get some professional help because your kids need both of you.

Principle #2: The Opossum

Growing up, I lived in a house that backed onto a canyon that was full of wildlife. It was a great place to grow up because my brothers and I used to go down into the canyon and play for hours. We came across all kinds of animals including raccoons, owls, slugs, and we even woke up one morning to find a cougar in our neighbor's back yard. One day when I was about 14, I was in the back yard and we came across an opossum that had obviously been injured in a fight with something much bigger. A big chunk of flesh had been taken out of it's back, its tail had almost fallen off, and it was limping heavily. My dad came out and picked it up, put it into a box and brought it into our garage. We called Animal Control and waited for them to come to pick it up. At some point during the afternoon while we were waiting, I went back into the garage to see how it was doing. At first it hadn't heard me come in the room and so it was trying to get out of the box. When I turned on the light, it froze and fell over backwards and didn't move. I freaked! I thought I had killed the thing by giving it a heart attack. My dad came running down the hall as I yelled for him. I think he thought it was attacking me. When I explained what had happened, he explained the concept of "playing possum". He told me that if I was quiet and left it alone, I would see that it would get back up. He was right.

A lot of times we as parents recognize that we need to change our children's behaviour, but we almost become afraid of them. We play possum with our own kids. We lay down and play dead, allowing them to decide what will happen in situations where we need to be a parent. We freeze and end up doing nothing saying something like, "well what am I supposed to do about it?"

I'm baffled by the shift that we have had in our society where parents are actually afraid of upsetting their kids. It happened somewhere and sometime, but one thing that's clear is that it's becoming an epidemic.

Here's a prime example. I was working with a father who had a 14-year-old son that was having some real problems with getting his homework done. His son would come home from school, go into his room and lock his door and spend the next 6-8 hours playing video games, collapsing in his bed at about 1 in the morning. This happened every day. The parents came to me and said that they were worried that his behaviours were going to have an impact on his ability to graduate. No kidding. When they asked me what to do, my question was, "What is it that's causing the problems?" They said that the Xbox was the biggest problem and they wished they could just get rid of it. My natural follow-up question was why didn't they do what they wished they could do. "Well, can you imagine how mad he would get?" I almost choked. "......And? I mean, unless the kid is going to come after you with a knife or something like that, what is wrong with occasionally making them upset?"

One thing we have to get past as parents is the notion that we have no power. It's like we are being run by the schoolyard bully. I once worked with a boy who was the target of bullying. He was in the fifth grade. At the time he was smaller than much of the class and there was one boy in his class that I swear had been shaving since the first grade. He was huge! And he chose the small guy to pick on. This young man came to me with tears in his eyes one day and said, "I don't know what to do! He punches me every day, he trips me on the school ground, and he calls me names. What do I do?" I dug deep into my bag of tricks with years of training to come up with the following. "Turn around and punch him as hard as you can, square in the nose and see if you can break his nose. As a matter of fact, if you punch him as hard as you can, I'll give you ten dollars". In hearing this, his mother went sheet white. "I'm not sure I agree with that". "That's fine. You don't have to agree. He doesn't have to do it. However, I promise that he won't get in trouble because I'll call the teacher and the principal myself and let them know what he's going to do and that I was the one who told him to do it."

You have to understand something here. The one and only reason that I suggested this for this young man is because I knew that in a normal situation he wouldn't hurt a fly. I'm in no way advocating that you or your child be encouraged to punch everyone in the face that you meet that offers you resistance because this isn't the point. The point was that someone else had the power and he felt like he could do nothing to stop it. The next time I saw him, he walked up to me and simply held out his hand, palm up with a big grin on his face. And he has never been bullied since.

The principle behind my suggestion to that young man to punch the bully in the face is the understanding is that if you believe you have no control, you really don't. We as parents in fact have a lot of control. Maybe not in what our teens do, but in how we choose to react to them. We have to believe that we have the right to outline what will go on in our houses.

As a parent, occasionally our job is to say "no", but again, how do we do that in a way that doesn't involve the wooden spoon in the kitchen drawer? I want to propose something that is the 3rd and final philosophy that I've seen parents take when it comes to dealing with negative behaviour. I call it, "Bowling for Dummies".

Principle #3: Bowling for Dummies

If you are like President Obama (see Jay Leno interview, March 18th, 2009) and me, you're not very good at bowling. Even with the Wii, my kids kick my butt every time I bowl. My elementary school aged daughter is serious competition to me. Sad. Do you want to know a secret that gets me more points when I bowl? I cheat. I go up to the attendant and say something like, "You know, I think my daughter would have much more fun if we could get those little bumper things in the gutters. Can you do that for her?" For her? Right!

If you think about a bowling alley that has the bumpers up, in between the bumpers there's space to move around. If you're like me, you may hit one or two pins on occasion. If you're like my kids, you hit all of them and then turn around to smirk at your dad. However, if the path you are on is too far off course, you hit the bumper and bounce back into the middle. Raising a teen is exactly the same thing. Your teens need to know what's expected and what's not acceptable so they can be bounced back into the middle.

Teens need and actually like to have clearly defined expectations to follow. Believe it or not. We all do. Think about the road. We have little marks of paint that tell us where we can go and where we can't go. It makes us feel safe. Have you ever driven through a construction zone where the pavement is being re-done or has been ripped out so there is no middle line? People freak out! They hit their brakes, pull as far over to the right as they can, they crawl along at 5-10 miles per hour, white knuckling it all the way. We all like to know "This is my area and when I'm in it, I'm safe".

The buzzword for this kind of parenting is "setting boundaries". Boundaries are synonymous with "expectations". I actually prefer expectations to boundaries because "boundaries" suggests that there is some leeway whereas expectation is what we expect. I expect the sun will rise tomorrow. Now, an expectation is not, "You do this without question". It is "You have this much give, after that there is no give."

Most of the literature out there on parenting says that expectations need to be consistent throughout life. That would mean that the assumption is that you have set and clarified expectations while your children were children. But they're not children anymore. Because of that, the rules need to change and so do the expectations.

Expectations can be defined as measurable, previously agreed upon limits to what's acceptable. They can't be nebulous like, "we expect you to be good". What the heck does that mean? Define good. Where do you stand on drugs? Sex (yes, you do need to talk about sex, even with your daughters)? Dating? Curfew? Grades in school? Computer use? Video games? Music and movies? Cell phone use? The list can obviously go on. Added to that, new things will come up as you experience new situations in life so you can't think of this as a once only exercise. I would EXPECT (sorry for the pun) that you would have this conversation with your teen multiple times throughout their lives with you and into their adulthood.

I'm going to make an assumption about your expectations. I'm going to assume that your teens know what the expectations are on some things already. Don't assume that that doesn't mean you don't need to talk about what they are though. It's important to be clear and concise about what you expect because your teen's actions will reflect the clarity. "You never said that" means you weren't very clear. Therefore, before you even approach your teen to go over your expectations, you need to be clear yourself on what it is you expect.

These expectations need to be laid out in a format with your teen that makes sense to both of you. Probably the best tool that I can think of is a contract between you and your teen. Life is all about agreements, and more often than not these agreements are done through a contract. So what does a contract with your teen look like?

Principle #4: Deal Or No Deal?

This is not a topic that most people would think would be in a chapter about discipline. There is a widely held misunderstanding that "discipline" means correcting behaviour and stopping something that has already happened. Although that's part of it, there's more to it than that.

A contract can be one of the most rewarding and effective tools in working with teens, but it can also be one of the most destructive pieces of paper ever created if done poorly. Everyone knows what a contract is. It's an agreement between two or more parties outlining expectations for both sides. Contracts are involved in just about every aspect of our lives. The homes we live in were arranged through a contract. The jobs that we have very often are subject to contracts. Even when you pay the waitress for lunch with your credit card, you're signing that you agree to the terms of the restaurant withdrawing that amount from your account. Contracts are a vital part of our lives, but I wonder how many people actually write contracts with their teens. Why not? It works well for everything else. Here are some simple steps that you can do to make a useful contract with your teen. Some families have actually found it useful to print these off and agree to them as rules as they are working through this process.

1) Start with the Non-Negotiables.

A long time ago I learned that when you're going to your boss to ask for a raise, ask for time off, or generally to ask for anything, do it on a Monday. Do NOT do it Friday afternoon. Why? Because people are more likely to say yes to things that are presented to them first before they get tired.

There are going to be certain things that you really want to get across. There are some that are not quite as important. Save those for the last.

2) Ask For Their Opinion

For every thing that you present, ask them what they think about it. As I have said before though, when you ask for their opinion on anything, be prepared to not like the opinion. The reason that you ask what they think about it is because this will engage them in the conversation as opposed to telling them what they will do. Again, remember that nobody (including you) likes to be told what they're going to do. You don't want to create a Donkeys-R-Us situation.

3) Be Flexible/Look for Options

You're going to get some resistance. Guaranteed. If you don't, you're probably either making them feel like their hands are being forced by not asking for their opinion effectively, or you have a kid that's from Mars. Resistance is good. It means that you're giving them space to come up with the solution to the problems at hand. It's an opportunity for you to talk and see if there are some alternatives to the proposal. As parents, we need to be creative and flexible when we're doing contracts, so don't hold too tight to your ideal. If they feel that 10 pm is too early to be home on weeknights and should be able to stay out to 11 (or whatever), what about 10:30? When working with teens, always remember that control is an illusion. Compromise works wonders.

4) Avoid Contempt/Respect Them

I spoke before about contempt. It's that feeling of "I'm better and smarter than you because I'm the adult". It's destructive and will detract from any conversation faster than anything else that happens. Really, we need to be adults here. We don't have space to sit in the corner and pout because our teen disagrees with what we're proposing. Get over it and grow up. We need to respect that they have opinions and have some level of insight into the situation at hand. Remember, "that's an option" is always an option.

5) Reverse the Process

Now it's their turn. Be ready again to not necessarily like what you hear, but respect their views the same way that you wanted them to respect yours. Look for alternatives, and work towards an agreement.

6) Sign It

Self-explanatory. Give them a copy of the agreement for their use and refer to it often whenever there are disagreements about what each side needs to do.

The Dark Side of Contracts

There's another side to this process. This is the destructive side of contracts. I saw a family once trying to create a contract where they didn't follow the steps above and it went very wrong. Mom and dad sat on one side of the table and the teen sat on the other, facing them like a firing squad. They began by saying, "Okay, here are the things that we expect of you." Then came about 20 items that were not requests, they were demands. "You WILL be home by 10 o'clock every night. You WILL do your laundry on your own every Saturday morning before you go anywhere…" etc. At no point did they ask for the opinion of their son. At no point did they notice his eye rolling and obvious frustration. Then they said to him, "Okay, what do you want?" He started with, "How about you aren't allowed to go into my room without me giving you permission?" His father said, "Look, I pay the mortgage so I will go into any room that I choose whenever I choose". I think they agreed to let him listen to his stereo for half an hour while he did his homework. They then swept the papers across the table and said, "Sign". This wasn't a contract. This was a forced confession. What did this kid learn? He learned that his parents didn't care about what he wanted, they didn't respect him, and they didn't trust him. This exercise did nothing more than deepen the rift between them. The potential for attachment turned into "get me out of here!"

Contracts Done Right

Why do I think contracts are so amazing? First of all, they eliminate the guesswork on your part and the part of your teen as to what the other side is expecting. Neither you or your teen can come back and say, "You never said that". Yes I did. It's right here. Second, it teaches a real life lesson. It tells them that they have responsibilities that need to be followed, but the benefits are also laid out for them. You have just provided the bumpers on the side of the bowling alley for them. They know what to expect and so do you. It's a simple and easy way to smooth things out before they happen and deepen the feeling that you are willing to listen and really care and respect them. Attachment anyone?

As I said, I love contracts. Discipline is not just correcting what happened, it's providing direction for what's about to happen. Once again, you're not yelling at them for using the wrong club while they're playing the game. You're saying, "See the green? How are you going to get there?"

Principle #5: Bouncing Them Back

In the last principle, I stated that it's our job to help bounce your teen back into the middle of the bowling alley. Often when I tell parents to "bounce them back into the middle", I hear, "I've tried everything and nothing works". They've tried threatening, they've tried taking away privileges, "time outs" stopped working when the teens realized that they can actually get up off of the stairs or open the door to their bedroom, and screaming obviously does nothing. The obvious question is, "What else is there?" There's one tool that I've found that relieves all of the pressure and "bad guy" stigma from you as a parent, and it really, really works. Why? Because you're letting them get out onto the playing field of football and allowing them to feel that the game can hurt sometimes and they begin to realize (make connections in the thinking part of the brain) that "maybe I should stop bashing my head against the wall".

Natural Consequences

Whatever your religious belief is, the best example of someone helping His children grow is God. Think about it. He has expectations for us, but He won't force us to follow them. Remember that the Ten Commandments are not multiple choice, but He isn't going to force you to follow them. He says, "Here it is. Take it or leave it." He has designed rules like gravity, tides, weather patterns, and others that all must be followed. If we try to break them, He doesn't necessarily stand over us and say, "I've told you not to do that! Listen to me!" He stands back as we decide to jump out of a tree and lets the rules take over, shakes his head and says, "Well that was dumb". It's a natural process. Everything that goes up must come down. I think we as parents need to take a page out of God's book when it comes to "bouncing our children back". Let me give you an example from the Bible.

God created Adam to take care of the Garden of Eden. Now, I want you to understand something. Adam's job was to take care of a garden that was always being watered, had no weeds, had no Big Mac containers laying around to pick up, and the garden was full of trees and plants that spontaneously produced fruit. Sign me up! However, because his job was so difficult, God sent in Eve to give him a hand. After He had these two wandering around the Garden for a while, He decided it was time to sit them both down and go over the rule. The one rule. He felt it was important enough to talk about because they may not know what the expectation was. In other words, He created a contract with them. This is what I imagine their conversation may have been like.

God: "Don't!"

Adam: "Don't what?"

God: "Don't touch the fruit of that tree"

Adam: "That one?"

God: "Yes, that one"

Adam: "...Is it any good?"

God: "Adam, focus on what I'm saying here."

Adam: "But why can't we eat it?"

God: "It's a natural law. The law says that if you do, I'm going to have to kick you out".

Adam: "So don't touch the fruit on that tree because if we do, you'll have to kick us out?"

God: "Exactly!"

Adam: "Got it!"

God went away from the Garden for a period of time and then decided He should come back and take a look at how things were going. When He got back, He saw Adam and Eve sitting down to a lovely meal of "forbidden fruit". I can just imagine Adam and Eve with the juice running down their mouths looking up at God, trying to smile and hide the fruit behind their backs. What did He do? He let the natural consequences take over. He had to.

The best way to understand what a natural consequence is for your teen is to put yourself into the teen's place. If you decided to stay up late and party one night and then had to go to work in the morning, what would happen? You would go to work the next day, perform poorly, and look like an idiot in your meetings. If you had to be at a hotel by 10pm or they would be closed with the doors locked, what would happen if you showed up at 10:45? Oh well, I guess you would have to sleep on the steps or find some other place to sleep. If you had a hard time with distractions but needed to get a project done for work, what would you do? You would remove all distractions and then have to wait to do what you wanted to do so you could do what needed to be done.

I saw a T.V. show once where a teenage girl would get mad at her parents over and over again. Each time, she would stomp out of the room and go upstairs to her room and slam the doors, shaking the house and knocking pictures off the wall. One time she started to stomp up the stairs and the camera focused on the family. Everyone except for the dad cringed, waiting for the earthquake. The dad smiled and went back to sipping his soup happily. The bang never came. Why? He had taken the door off of the hinges and put it into the garage before the fight had happened. No door, no problem.

Take Away the Take Aways

One of the biggest mistakes that I see parents making when they're trying to implement the natural consequences is thinking that a natural consequence means that you need to take something away. Although that may sometimes be the response, it isn't the first and last line of defense.

There was a family that met with me for quite some time a few years ago. When I first met them, they said that their son didn't respect them and that they had tried everything to get him to listen. When I asked what that meant, they said that they had taken literally everything away from him. He was now sleeping in his completely bare room with only a blanket to keep him warm. I asked for examples of some of the reasons they had taken away things from him. Their answers startled me. The reason that his bed had been taken away was because he had hit his brother with a toy that they had been fighting over. They took away his bike from him because he refused to apologize for saying that the dinner his mother had cooked for him smelled like something the dog left out in the back yard. His favorite hat had been taken away because he chose not to hand in an assignment in math. And they had no idea when he was going to get it all back.

If you look at these examples, not one of the consequences is related to the action. It's like saying to you, "I'm going to take away your car because you chose to go to TGI Friday's instead of KFC to pick up my dinner." Huh? What does that teach? Not much other than the world makes no sense whatsoever. It also teaches a sense of helplessness for both the parent and the teen that I have often seen lead into further problems that are much harder to fix. It has been my experience that this rarely works the way the parents hope it will. On top of that, kids are pretty adept and figuring out alternatives. If you take away the computer or the Playstation, they always have a friend who has one that they can go and visit.

The natural consequence is one that is directly related to the behaviour. And more often than not, the best and most effective consequences are not ones that you impose on them. They are the ones that life imposes on them. Don't be afraid to let your teen fail a class if they're spending too much time hanging out with friends. Unless your child sincerely needs help, failing a class or even a grade is a great natural consequence. Don't be afraid to let your teen be locked out of the house because they're out past curfew. Unless it's minus twenty degrees out, they probably won't die. They might be cold, but they probably won't be late for curfew too often after that. We have to get over needing to protect them from the outside world and feeling like we have no power in a situation. We have an immense amount of power. We have the power to choose not to protect them when life is trying to teach them a lesson. And remember, we all have to experience negative in life to learn from it.

Summary

- There are many things that work and many that don't when disciplining your teen.

- Recognize that you do have the right to say "no", and making them mad is okay sometimes.

- Set expectations and let them know verbally what they are.

- When they hit the bumpers, bounce them back into the middle.

Chapter 7: Am I doing a good job as a parent?

In short…probably.

Most parents that I meet are really trying. I've met and worked with just about every type of parent out there. I've worked with the multi-millionaire CEO parents, the blue collar work your fingers to the bone parents, the middle management parents, and the drug dealing gang bangers. If they're sitting in front of me, they care. They want to know how to do better.

As men, most of us feel that what it takes to be a man is the ability to take care of our children and families. That's why one of the biggest reasons behind dads abandoning their families is the feeling that they can't provide financially for them. In truth, there's no scale to determine if you're doing "good enough" as a parent.

In all of my years working with families, I've learned that there are three things that make an effective parent. They are 1) compassion, 2) honesty, and 3) the ability to say, "I'm sorry". To what degree each of these are implemented is completely up to you.

Many people I've met would say that these three things, compassion, honesty, and the ability to sincerely apologize are contrary to what it means to be a man. In my research I've come across various individuals throughout the years who say that a real man is someone who is tough, strong, shows no emotion, and has lots of sex. Now, the last one may not be too bad, but if people truly believe that those other things are solely what make up the definition of "man", they need a real adjustment, or as Zig Ziglar would say, "They have a serious case of 'Stinkin Thinking'".

What's great about this is that nobody in the world can tell you if you're doing a good job as a parent. Could you do better? Always. But you're the one who measures whether you're doing a *good enough* job. I said it before. There's no way to be a perfect parent, but there are a million ways to be a great parent. So here's an outline of what I use to determine how I'm doing.

Principle #1: Compassion

Compassion can be defined as the true love of Christ. When He was on the earth, Jesus embodied compassion. The Bible is replete with examples of Jesus' compassion for sometimes complete strangers. Compassion is more than just caring for others. It's being so sensitive to the needs of the other that we can sense when they're having problems and we're driven to help them.

I once spoke to a father whose daughter was put into a situation where she had to call the police for assistance. Once she had called the police, she called her father who was a few hours away to come and get her. He was hours away by car, but there wasn't a moment of hesitation when he heard his daughter's voice on the other end of the phone. He walked out of the meeting he was in, had his assistant cancel the rest of his appointments for the day and went out to get her. Once he finally made it there, the police officer who attended called him to check and see how his daughter was doing. In relating this story to me, the father said, "And then the police officer said the stupidest thing I think I've ever heard. He said, 'Thank you for coming all the way out here to pick her up'. Can you believe it? He thanked me for doing my job as a father. What was I going to do? Let her sit here when she needed me?"

It has been my experience that most of the parents I've met have compassion for their children. It's a drive that we have been given as humans to love and serve those in our care. This drive is a blessing, but it's also a curse in the same breath. Why do you think you get so frustrated with your teens? Why did I call this book, "How to Raise a Teenager Without Using Duct Tape" and not "The Wonderful and Blissful Years of Raising Teenagers"? Was it because I needed a catchy title that had no relevance whatsoever to raising teens? No! It was because at times we want to use the whole box of tape to wrap them up in, tie them to the front bumper, and drive through rush hour traffic without using the brakes. Why? Because we care so much for them. Really. Think about it. Think about everything that I've said throughout this whole book about what it's like for you to try to learn to back off, to fight the urge to take over, the urge to make decisions for them. You do it because you're scared to death for them. You love them so much that you want them to succeed with as little harm as possible.

When people say that men have no emotions outside of anger, they are so, so wrong. Men actually have as much emotion as women, but what's accepted in society is anger, so that's the "F" word that we naturally default to. We fight. But as a parent, you don't have to fight. It's a choice that you make. Every time you get angry, you've made the choice to get angry. Every time that you get happy, you've made the choice to be happy. When you're dealing with your children, make the choice to show compassion. Make the choice to get down to their level and remember how much it absolutely sucked to be a teenager. Remember how their brains still need time to develop and so some of the stupid things they're doing are honestly not their fault. They have to learn. Have compassion for these little half-brained teens because you were one at some time as well. Choose compassion.

Principle #2: Honesty

There are two types of honesty that are important in dealing with our children. The first is honesty in what we do and say. The second is honesty in what we are experiencing in life.

Monkey see…

I had been working with Sarah for about 6 months. She was the typical punk teen who pretended like she didn't care what anyone said and she would do what she wanted when she wanted. In the school she was ruthless. She wasn't a big kid, but she went out of her way to ally herself with those who could do her dirty work for her. People avoided her in the halls and she was in the school office more often than she saw the inside of a classroom. But it was all an act. It was funny to me to see Sarah come into the room with her hat on sideways, her hair in her eyes, and great me with her traditional "Wassup?" She would plunk herself down on the chair and slouch back looking at me through the wisps of hair in her eyes. After about 5 minutes though, 90% of the time she would sit up a little bit more, sweep the hair out of her eyes and sometimes I actually saw her head without a hat on it. We talked about her act and she said that she had to act like that to survive her life. I assumed that it meant her school life, but I got a phone call one morning that changed all of that.

One morning her mom called and said that she had been kicked out of school for selling drugs there. She had forgotten to lock her locker properly that day and her friend got in and stole some of the drugs…in front of a teacher. Apparently they only had brainiacs at this school. The teacher opened the locker and found enough drugs to kill a horse. The police were called and they were wondering what I thought should happen to her. I went over to the school and met Sarah in an office in handcuffs. In attendance were her dad, her mom, the police, and her principal. When I got there, her dad was yelling at her saying, "How long do think you could have gotten away with this? You know how we feel about drugs, and now you've totally embarrassed us. What were you thinking?" While everyone was in the room, she acted like the punk (we actually called the act "The Bag Lady") that everyone expected her to. I asked everyone in the room to excuse us and when they left, all of a sudden Sarah broke down. I had never seen her quite so emotional. Part of it was fear, but what blew me away was what she said to me. "That #@$^%! He stands there and tells me 'we don't believe in drugs' but he has a grow-op in his friend's barn that he thinks nobody knows about! And he says I've embarrassed him?" This father stood in the room and berated his daughter for doing something that he himself was doing. She had every right to be mad at him.

As parents, we don't have the liberty to say one thing and then do the other. We can't expect our children to be something that we're not. Research shows that a large portion of what makes up who we are is what we learn from our parents or caregivers. Again, your kids aren't stupid. More often than not they really do know what you're doing. Don't pretend to be something you're not. Reading this, some parents may think, "well, I don't have a grow-op so I am fine". It may be true that this example doesn't apply, but if we want our children to be honest with us, honesty must permeate everything that we do and say to our children.

Being Afraid to Say "I Don't Know".

In my research, I met with a father and we were discussing the principle of honesty and he told me a great story. He said, "As a family, we have our computer on the main floor. It's something that we've always done because we know that a computer in the bedroom can lead to some really scary things. Often while the girls are on the computer my wife or I will walk up behind them, not to check up on them necessarily, but to see what they are up to. One day my 14 year old daughter was sitting on the computer doing her chat thing. I will never understand how they can chat with 15 people at one time. As I came up behind her, all of a sudden I saw her shutting down the windows as quickly as she could. I freaked out! I said, 'What are you doing?' She responded just as quickly, 'Nothing!' I definitely didn't get what I wanted, which was information. I wanted to know who she was talking to and why she didn't want me to know. I also realized that I needed to take another approach because she had shut the door on me. I took a deep breath and said something like, 'I'm sorry. I shouldn't have snapped at you like that. Let me tell you what just happened. I was walking up here and I saw you shutting down all of those windows and I got worried. I know you're smart and know how dangerous the internet is, but I guess my inner dad came out and I was scared for you. I just want to make sure you're safe. Can you help me to feel safe and let me know why you felt you needed to shut down all the windows?'"

I've used this story before and some parents have said, "That sounds totally fake! I would never say anything like that." That's fine. I'm not suggesting that you copy the above script and stand in front of your teen and read it like a bed-time story. Take the principle of, "I'm feeling...and I don't know what to do with it" and adapt it to your language.

Another time where honesty is crucial is during times of trial. When tragedy strikes in a family, or there are challenges that the family is facing, I've sometimes heard parents say, "Maybe we shouldn't tell them the whole story. Maybe spare the details". I have some good friends whose baby was ill and they were told by doctors that he would likely not live very long. The parents were obviously distraught and felt like they should withhold the fact that they could lose the baby from the other children. For what? To spare them from worrying? Let's be honest. You aren't sleeping, you're emotional, you're going to the doctor on a regular basis, and maybe arguing more. The kids know something is going on and they're already worrying, even if they don't vocalize it. By withholding your true feelings and fears, your children will be faced with a bit of a dilemma. They know what they're feeling, but you're telling them that what they're feeling is wrong. "Don't worry. It'll all be okay." But what if it won't? This goes back to the principle of protecting your teens. At some point, the padding will come off and they'll have to face the fact that maybe it isn't going to be okay.

Please understand, in no way am I making light of suffering. It is a horrible fact of life that sometimes we're faced with realities where hurt and pain can sometimes feel unbearable. But your teens need to hear it. They need to hear you say that you're scared, hurt, angry, sad, or whatever the situation may be. For one reason. Because it's okay to feel those things. When you're honest about how you truly feel, your teens will know that it's okay to feel these things and they'll be more willing in the future to share THEIR feelings with YOU. It's an interesting contradiction that sometimes it takes great courage to say "I'm scared". But it's honest and your teens will follow suit and be more honest with you.

Principle #3: I'm Sorry

My daughter has a face that projects everything she feels. I'll strongly suggest to her that she not consider a career as a poker player because she wouldn't be able to handle it if she got a good hand. Everyone would fold in an instant.

In chapter 3, I talked about triggers. One of my triggers is when I come home at the end of the day and my wife is stressed out because the kids have done something (or several things) to make her consider very strong alcohol. One day, I came home after a particularly hard day with my clients. I was tired, hungry, and needed some peace and quiet. As I put the alarm on my car, I heard the screaming. My wife and daughter were going at each other for something my daughter had done. I really don't even remember what it was. I came into the house and my wife met me at the door-step. Before I had time to fully turn the handle to come inside, my wife regaled me with stories about these children who must have come from Satan and how she couldn't take one more minute of it. I went in and found that my daughter had barricaded herself in her room and refused to let me in. Once I finally got in, she informed me that she didn't want to talk and then covered her ears and closed her eyes. I blew. I started yelling and threatening her. When she opened her eyes, the look on her face stabbed me right in the heart. She was so hurt that I yelled at her that she curled up in the corner and just wailed. I had really screwed up. I took a deep breath and collected myself and then went to sit next to her on the bed. I put my arms around her and started rocking her. Once she and I had calmed down enough, I said, "Sweetheart, I'm sorry. I really got mad and I made the mistake of yelling at you. I'm so sorry."

"I am sorry" can be the 3 strongest words that we can ever use with our children. That and "I love you". A sincere apology will melt hearts and create bonds between us and our children that are rock-solid. Unfortunately sometimes men can be stubborn and we find it hard to say those words to our children. We sometimes take the attitude of "I'm the dad and so shouldn't have to apologize. They should've listened in the first place". If you believe that, then you might need to go back to the beginning of this book and read it again.

We need to suck it up. We need to stop being so stubborn and immature and accept the fact that we screw up…a lot.

John Gottman, who I have mentioned previously, calls these conversations "stress reducing conversations. When couples come to see me, more often than not what I hear about is what the other person has done to bring them to this point. The ones who come in and say, "You know what? I did this, and this, and that. In a lot of ways the reason we're here is because of me" are the ones who generally only have to see me a few times. In all the years I've been working with families, I can think of four people off of the top of my head who have actually come in with this approach. Four! We are so quick to find fault in the other person that we forget to take a look at "The Man in the Mirror" as the late Michael Jackson would suggest. Why is it so hard to admit we're wrong? Personally I think it's our egos. Suck it up buttercup. You're at least fifty percent to blame for every single situation that you find yourself in, positive or negative. Relationships are never one-sided and so the next time you start to fight with your teen (or anyone for that matter) ask yourself, "What have I contributed to this situation?" When you come up with the answer, turn around to your teen and apologize for your portion of the situation. Be clear, concise and don't make excuses for what you've done. You messed up. Sorry about that. I'll try to do better next time.

Principle #4: Real Men Wear Pink

I don't necessarily want to get all touchy-feely here, but I want to stress why this book was written with dads in mind. The challenge that men have in our North American society regarding raising our teens is that we're facing an immense bias about what we can and can't do. I would say that a large percent of our problems come from the idea that men don't know what they're doing and that they aren't as responsible for the rearing of our children as women. GENERALLY SPEAKING. I know there's an exception to every rule, but we as men have bought that crap. I think it's time to start asking "why?" Why do we believe that, and what effect is that belief having on our relationships with our children, our partners, and our society in general?

It's our responsibility, our right, our blessing (or curse depending on the glasses you choose to wear) to be actively engaged in our children's lives from the time that they're born until the day we die. We need to get over the feeling of insecurity in having heart to heart discussions with our teens and opening up about how we really feel. Your insecurity isn't your family's fault. It's yours, so don't let them suffer because you feel "weird talking about this kind of stuff". You are so missing out! Your kids need you to learn to be comfortable with the uncomfortable. They need you to change the view of "man". I'm confident that if we all took the time to explore how we could get a bit uncomfortable, our society would change. Call me an idealist, but the last time I checked, pacifists that have an impact on the world like Gandhi are few and far between.

Summary

- Nobody can tell you how you're doing. It's all up to how you feel you're doing.

- Compassion is the ability to put yourself in the other person's shoes and put their needs before yours.

- You can't expect your teen to be honest with you unless you're the picture of honesty yourself.

- "I'm sorry". Learn it. Feel it. Say it. Often.

Chapter 8: Summary to the Summary of the Summaries

Parents have often asked me, "What's the secret to raising my child so that I don't want to kill them?" Honestly, that question often highlights the biggest problem. You're not raising a child anymore. You're raising a teenager. Because of that, everything that you've learned to this point about raising kids needs to be thrown out because it won't work. You can no longer hold their hand and lead them down the path. Your job now is to step back and ask them where they want to go and then help them decide how they're going to get there. This is done by being there for them when they want to talk, allowing them to get mad, and understanding that they really only have half a brain (well, okay…two-thirds of a brain).

Being an effective parent also means that you have to be aware of what's going on for you. Often times we get frustrated with our teens when the fault really isn't theirs. Something inside of us has gone on that brings out levels of emotion and we end up taking them out on our kids. They have enough problems as it is without having to deal with ours. We need to step back and take responsibility for what's ours and then control it. Without that awareness, we're useless when it comes to setting limits and expectations.

We have to be okay with stepping back a little and letting life do the talking. The best lessons often will not come from you. Life does a good job of smacking us around and it usually has more impact when we learn it ourselves. Don't tell them life doesn't hurt just to protect them. Reality is often less painful when we expect things in life to hurt a little bit.

Having said that, you have every right to say, "No" and set some expectations. Life has some "no's" in it, so your teen's going to have to learn that at some point. Give your teen the opportunity to understand the expectations before you get into the situation if you can and get their agreement. It's a lot easier to accept reality if we have agreed to it. Contracts can be an incredible tool if they're done right.

You're doing a good job. Really. Most parents kind of chuckle when I say that because none of us feels like we deserve the accolades. Some days, I feel like the worst dad in the world. I'm not sure about you, but my life doesn't very closely reflect a 1950's sitcom. But on the whole, we're all doing the best with what we have. We all have lots to learn and only you can judge how well you're doing. Remember that being comfortable is never a good thing. You have to go outside of what's comfortable to be the kind of parent that you want to be. Leave the comfort for your favorite pair of jeans.

Finally, remember that we're all faking it. None of us really knows what we're doing. The sooner you come to terms with that, the sooner I expect that you will find more creative ways for using that box of duct tape you keep in the garage…"just in case".

Take care, and I hope to see you out on the course someday standing back watching our kids play the game.

About the Author

Jay Timms BMT, MA, CCC is a Relationship and Family Counsellor, author, Music Therapist, and Founder and President of the on-line educational and life coaching company Jay Timms.com. Jay's award winning research exploring the relationship between fathers and their teenage children has shed light on the impact of positive attachments throughout the lives of children and how fathers can play a vital role in a teen's development. Jay's direct approach allows clients to see alternatives to their current life situations.

Jay works with adults and youth who face a variety of challenges. Having worked within school districts throughout British Columbia, Canada, and for the Province of British Columbia as a Mental Health Consultant to Child Welfare with The Ministry of Children and Family Development, Jay is aware of many of the challenges facing youth and teens. Being a parent, husband, and previous business executive, Jay is also keenly aware of the challenges facing individuals who are burdened by daily stresses of life and just can't seem to get out of the "rut".

When Jay isn't at the office, he enjoys spending time playing musical instruments, photography, skiing and snowboarding, riding his motorcycle, traveling, and "hanging out" with his wife and 2 children.